"Finally, the secrets to the supernatural are revealed for the greatest miracle ministry I have investigated—Kathryn Kuhlman! Why now? Because God is ready to do it again!"

SID ROTH
Host, *It's Supernatural!* television

Healing
IN HIS
Presence

OTHER BOOKS BY JOAN GIESON

Things Thought Impossible

Prayers and Promises for Healing

Healing
IN HIS
Presence

The Untold Secrets of

KATHRYN KUHLMAN'S HEALING MINISTRY
AND RELATIONSHIP WITH HOLY SPIRIT

JOAN GIESON

DESTINY IMAGE® PUBLISHERS, INC.
P.O. Box 310, Shippensburg, PA 17257-0310
"Promoting Inspired Lives."

This book and all other Destiny Image and Destiny Image Fiction books are available at Christian bookstores and distributors worldwide.

Cover design by Eileen Rockwell
Cover photo by John Denniston
Interior design by Terry Clifton

For more information on foreign distributors,
call 717-532-3040.

Reach us on the Internet: www.destinyimage.com.

ISBN 13 TP: 978-0-7684-1414-1
ISBN 13 eBook: 978-0-7684-1415-8
ISBN 13 HC: 978-0-7684-1467-7
ISBN 13 LP: 978-0-7684-1466-0

For Worldwide Distribution, Printed in the U.S.A.
1 2 3 4 5 6 7 8 / 21 20 19 18 17

Contents

A Word from the Publisher

From the moment I heard Joan Gieson speak on Sid Roth's *Miracle Explosion* program with Joan Hunter and Clarice Fluitt, I knew she had to share *this* book with the world!

Joan is a powerful minister, evangelist, and agent of compassion in her own right. In fact, I spent several hours sitting with her and her husband Frank, getting to know them and listening to stories about Kathryn Kuhlman. Amazing miracles. Bus rides to the miracle crusades filled with supernatural happenings. Secrets from behind closed doors of what kind of person Miss Kuhlman *really was* and how her walk with God in everyday life is what postured her to be saturated by the Spirit's presence on the platform.

As Joan shared several testimonies, wave after wave of the Holy Spirit's presence would come upon us as we all became undone by the amazing work of God. *Why?* Is it because Kathryn Kuhlman is some kind of spiritual superstar whom we need to write a book about, explaining why she was so unique and special? No—although I do believe she is a general who deserves great honor.

Here is what I got while interviewing Joan Gieson—Kathryn Kuhlman lived a life and enjoyed a relationship with the Holy Spirit that should be provoking to every single believer. It should be invitational and inclusive, not off limits and exclusive. This invitation extends to you! Miss Kuhlman was not unusually qualified. In fact, much happened in her life that should have naturally disqualified her. She was not perfect, nor did she present herself to be. She did not claim to have any kind of unique edge with God that was inaccessible to "everyday people."

Kathryn Kuhlman simply decided to give herself completely to the Holy Spirit and yield to His lordship in her life.

Get ready. Joan Gieson has offered a unique treasure of a book that gives you a behind-the-scenes look at Kathryn Kuhlman and how what she practiced in her walk with God is available and *transferable* to you!

This much I know—you will come to a very speedy conclusion. You will quickly see that the miracles and healings were not about Kathryn Kuhlman. They were not about Joan Gieson—who continues to witness a consistent demonstration of miracles in her life and ministry. It's not about some unique man or woman who has some healing "touch." It has everything to do with the healing *presence* of the Holy Spirit, the One who has been given to each of us by a good and gracious Father.

Here is the question that begins your journey: *how filled with His presence are you willing to be?* ★

LARRY SPARKS
Publisher, Destiny Image

INTRODUCTION

My time with Kathryn Kuhlman was amazing. The experiences and miracles and all the wonderful things that happened during my time with this great woman of God are forever etched into my mind. I'm excited to share those testimonies with you and begin with a bit of personal background that I hope you will find interesting, even amusing.

However, I believe it's important for you to read this chapter before you read anything else. Why? Not because Joan Gieson is someone important. Oh no, I'm not. I'm not unique. I'm not special. Sure, uniquely created by God and special to Him, but I am not qualified to be used by Him more than anyone else. My story could easily be your story. Even though our experiences are most certainly different and our personal stories vastly unique, the common denominator is God's purpose unfolding. He takes great joy in using the weak things of the world to confound the wise and displaying supernatural power through vessels of clay (see 1 Cor. 1:27; 2 Cor. 4:7).

In the following pages, you will get to know me a little more. This is not meant to be an autobiography about myself or even a biographical work about Miss Kuhlman. That's not my heart. The truth is, there are many wonderful books written about Kathryn Kuhlman, her life, her ministry, and her legacy. This book simply recounts my experience knowing this woman behind the scenes, watching her life, and witnessing her friendship with the Holy Spirit.

While I believe God only created one Kathryn Kuhlman—and He is not calling us to be copies of her, or others, when He has made us to be originals—I do believe that we all have much to learn from how this woman intimately and powerfully walked with the Holy Spirit. She did not present herself as spiritually superior to anyone else. Rather, I see her life as an invitation to whosoever would hunger and thirst to experience more of God.

There is more of God available to you, dear reader. More of His presence. More of His power. More of His glory. More of His character. More of His kindness. How do you experience *more*? It has everything to do with your relationship with this wonderful Person called the Holy Spirit. This was Kathryn's secret. While many focus on the miracles, it is a great delight for me to share about the *untold secrets* of Kathryn's life and ministry.

Once more, I don't share this information to offer a biographical sketch of Kathryn Kuhlman's life. Instead, I present to you a thrilling invitation of what could be possible in your life—a life that pays that most wonderful price to walk in the miraculous and watch God move in power before your eyes. I'll share a little of my personal story, yes, but I only do it to remind you that just as God has used Joan Gieson, an Italian woman from Jennings, Missouri, and Kathryn Kuhlman, a redhead from Concordia, Missouri, the same God can display His mighty miracle-working power through you too!

Part One

MY JOURNEY
with
KATHRYN KUHLMAN

Chapter 1

---•◦•---

DAYS TO REMEMBER

MY CHILDHOOD

I am an Italian woman from a simple Italian family with a mom and a dad and a sister and a brother. My father had a small produce stand on a corner in Jennings, Missouri. I can remember at two years old standing on that corner selling fruits and vegetables to passersby. At Christmas, we would sell Christmas trees and fruit and cranberries and all sorts of things that smelled really good. I was always part of whatever was going on. Perhaps that is why I enjoyed being part of Kathryn's ministry—there was always something wonderful going on.

My dad had an old Model T Ford truck, and he would fill it with those fruits and vegetables, and he would peddle his wares up and down the streets of our small, rural community. I would go with him, and at each house I'd jump out of the truck, which had no doors, and go knock on the doors. The person who came to the door wouldn't see me at first because I was little and short, but when the person, usually the woman of the home, looked down, there I was. When she opened the screen door, I handed her a little piece of paper that listed what we had for sale and the price—apples, two cents apiece, oranges, potatoes, and the like. The lady would check off what she wanted and I'd run down to the road and give it to my dad who was waiting at the truck. He'd fill the order and I'd deliver it with a great big smile.

At the end of the day, my mother would take a few of the leftover fruits and the vegetables and make something unbelievably wonderful out of them for dinner. Dad would keep track of the poorest of the poor we met each day, those who said they couldn't afford to buy any food. My dad never left those houses without giving them something to eat. In addition to his kindness at the time, at the end of the day, Dad would give Mom and me a little peach that had a sad spot in it, and we would make a cobbler. Or with a few vegetables we made a casserole and took it to the people who needed help.

So were our days filled! Giving was something I learned from my mother and father—it was a natural part of our lifestyle. And we never ate alone as a family of five—we always shared our meals with people who came to visit or maybe were just passing by.

HOUSE FULL OF LOVE

We were very poor and lived with seven people in a house that was 24 by 24 feet—Grandma and Grandpa, Mom and Dad, and three children. I was the oldest of the three. We children didn't realize we were poor; we thought we lived in a mansion. Everybody in the neighborhood came to our house—it was the local gathering place. After school, all my friends stopped by. There were always people inside and outside. I learned how to love those people—they were like family. Amazing how God was shaping me for my future in these tight, unimpressive quarters. Let this be a word of encouragement to you, dear one—no matter where you find yourself while reading these words, God Almighty is not put off by your upbringing, your background, or your lack (or abundance). God will work His mighty purposes in and through you regardless of your credentials, education, accolades, or influence. I had no idea that Heaven was so wonderfully directing my steps from the time I was a young girl, living in a cramped house with seven people. In those years, even before I knew Jesus, I believe the Lord was showing me how to love. If you want to walk in the miraculous, it all begins with love.

Love and giving were definitely present in those early years. I learned how to give because of my mom and dad. They weren't religious fanatics; they were just genuine, sincere people whose nature was to give love in whatever simple way possible. We belonged to a Missouri Synod Lutheran Church. I was baptized and raised in the church.

One day at school, I met my handsome husband-to-be. I noticed that the girls just loved Frank. They hugged him and kissed him and wanted to take him home to meet their parents. At the time, I had two girlfriends, and one of them Frank was in love with. The other he didn't like at all. The one he liked didn't like him, and the one he couldn't stand said she was going to kill herself if he didn't love her back and marry her. I was the neutral party in this triangle of shenanigans. Then all of a sudden one day when we were looking for the girl he really liked, he leaned over and kissed me! Can you imagine?! He kissed me, and right then I fell in love with him—that was more than sixty years ago.

Today we've been married for almost sixty years, and we have two children. We were married in October and our first son was born in November the following year. He was a perfect child, absolutely wonderful. Frank worked every day, and I worked every day, and we bought a home. Everything seemed so good.

SOME YEARS LATER

Some years later, I got sick and lost my sight. I don't remember the exact date, but I do remember it was the day Cassius Clay (Muhammad Ali) had a big fight scheduled. I was in the ophthalmology office and the doctor said to me, "You have hemorrhages behind both eyes, and the optic nerve is swollen into the brain. This is why you go blind at times." Then he said, "It could be permanent, and we think it's a tumor. We're going to have to investigate." So I was admitted to the hospital for examinations and tests. Off and on for about three years, I saw nine doctors and was admitted to ten hospitals. No one knew what exactly the problem was or how to solve it.

When I was in the hospital, my mom came over and took care of the house because every day I became progressively more and more ill until finally I was not able to do anything. Because I could lose my sight at any time and for any length of time, my activity was severely limited. I couldn't drive the car, for example. It was a very scary and uncertain time in my life and the life of my family.

A HOLY ROLLER

One day a beautiful lady who lived down the street came to our house. Out of all the houses on that street, this lady was the "religious one"—a "Holy Roller." Although everyone on the street went to church, none of us attended a "Holy Roller" church. (*Holy roller* was a derogative, condescending term used to describe full-gospel, Pentecostal churches at the time.)

Although I never missed a Sunday service in my church from the time I was born, one day this young lady with six kids came to my house and said to me, "Joan, I want to tell you about Jesus."

"Oh Louise, I know about Jesus. I haven't missed a Sunday for twenty-four years in my church," I said.

"No," she said, "I really want to share with you about Jesus."

"Okay, well...we'll do that another day," I said, because I thought she was a religious fanatic, and I really didn't want anything to do with that.

A few weeks later, it was the first day of school for our son Michael, who was six years old. I was determined to take him to school on the first day, but because the blindness was still coming and going, he had to take my hand. The teacher placed a chair outside the room so I could sit and relax for a while. As I sat there, all of a sudden I couldn't see; but in my spirit I heard my neighbor lady laughing and bouncing around. I also heard a bunch of little kids, and I knew she was walking up the same steps with her children that Michael and I had just walked up. Then I felt her pass me by. Although I couldn't see her, I felt her.

Then another minute or so went by and the teacher walked out of Michael's classroom and said, "Joan, Michael's sick. You're going to have to take him home." My grandfather was a char- ter member of the Lutheran church in Jennings,

Missouri, so everybody knew our family. I said, "Judy, I don't have a car. I don't drive any longer. We have to wait till noon when the bus comes and takes us home."

With that, there was a lady at my side saying, "I overheard the conversation, and I'll be glad to take you and your son home." On the way, the lady told me about Jesus, and I invited Jesus Christ into my heart and accepted Him as my Lord and Savior. Her name was Anne Richards, and she became my spiritual mother from that moment on. I was born again. Now my life was brand new. Even though I couldn't see naturally, I could see spiritually; and even though I couldn't focus on what I was doing all the time, I could focus on everything that was most important. My life changed! Physically I couldn't see, but spiritually I could see for the first time.

GET ME TO PITTSBURGH!

While lying in bed one day, I heard a woman say, "Hello there. Have you been waiting for me?" And I thought, *Wow! What a crackpot she is!* And I turned the radio off. The next day I'm right in the same spot waiting for Michael to come home on the bus and I hear the same voice, "Hello there. Have you been waiting...?" I turned off the radio again. The third day, I didn't hear the woman ask that question. In fact, I don't even remember how or when the radio was tuned in to that station. Now, of course, I know that God set the whole thing up.

This time I heard a woman say, "I was so sick. The doctor said I was going to die." She continued, "I went to a miracle service—and God healed me." I got up off the bed and pressed my ear to the speaker where I could hear the radio: "This broadcast is coming from the Kathryn Kuhlman Foundation in Pittsburgh, Pennsylvania."

I grabbed the telephone and dialed Frank's work number. "Frank, get home now and get me to Pittsburgh. Jesus is there right this second and I want you to take me to Pittsburgh so I can be healed," I blurted out as quickly as possible. He rushed home—and brought the pastor with him. He also brought my mother and my grandfather. They thought that whatever was wrong with me, it had gone too far and I had lost hold on reality.

"No, no, I heard it on the radio," I told them. "I can be healed!"

They listened to me, but eventually went back to whatever they were doing and left me alone. I thought, *I don't care what they say or think. I heard the truth and I know the truth.*

I found out more about the Katheryn Kuhlman Foundation and I asked Frank many times over the next few years to take me to Pittsburgh. There was a lady in our church, Shirley, who had multiple sclerosis and was really bad off. She couldn't walk. She was in a wheelchair. I asked Frank one more time, "Will you please take me to a Kathryn Kuhlman miracle service in Pittsburgh, Pennsylvania? And we've got to take Shirley with us." Richard, Shirley's husband, was agreeable, happy to have a few days free from having to care for his wife 24/7.

Frank gave in and had the guts to put us in his brand-new car and drove us all the way from St. Louis, Missouri to Pittsburgh, Pennsylvania—18 hours. He had to feed both of us. He had to take care of Shirley, even changing her diapers—not Pampers that are disposable, real cloth diapers that had to be washed and dried. Frank had to take care of all of that. When we arrived, we stood in front of the church all night long; Shirley sat in her wheelchair and we stood on the steps. Now mind you, I wasn't out of bed that long since the blindness began. Frank and I stood for hours listening to people singing who had come from Canada, New York, St. Louis, and many areas of Illinois. We were standing body-to-body close with a couple from Salina, Kansas. The woman had health problems too, so we shared our stories with each other. I told her I could see her while talking to her—but not all the time, as my vision came and went.

Then it seemed like all of a sudden 9 o'clock in the morning came and the doors opened, but Shirley was gone. We then realized that they had taken her over to a wheelchair section. I was sitting in the back of the church and I closed my eyes and started to cry. I didn't know why I was crying.

"Frank, there's a light on my head," I said.

"Joan, there's no light on your head."

"Frank, please tell them to turn the light off my head. I feel illuminated and everybody is looking at me."

"There's no one looking at you. There's no light on your head. Open your eyes," Frank said.

"I Can See!"

When I opened my eyes, I could see as well as the day I was born. All the blindness had gone. I could see so very clearly. All of the imbalance had disappeared. I was no longer a human being just trying to feel my way through life. I knew where I was. I could see!

"Frank, I can see!"

"No you can't, be quiet."

"Frank, I can see, I can see!"

"No, be quiet, honey, they're going to throw us out of here," Frank said.

Right then, Maggie, Miss Kuhlman's personal assistant, a tall, thin, beautiful lady, stopped at our aisle and said, "Has there been someone healed in this aisle?"

"Yes, it's me!" I exclaimed.

"What happened?" she asked.

"I couldn't see. I was blind and I have been for four years," I explained.

"What has happened?" Maggie asked again.

"I can see. I can see the entire church. I can see the stained-glass windows. I can see Miss Kuhlman. I can see. I can see!"

"Come on out. I want to take you down to Miss Kuhlman," Maggie said.

So I walked out into the aisle and Frank said, "I'm not going with you."

"Okay," I said.

Maggie and I started to walk down the center aisle, and when we got just a few feet, I heard Frank say, "Hold on, I'm right behind you." So the three of us walked toward Miss Kuhlman.

When we reached Miss Kuhlman, she had just raised her hand over the lady from Salina, Kansas, and down on the floor she went—overwhelmed by the power of God. She was healed. Then Miss Kuhlman turned to Frank and me. She never said a word; she merely lifted her hand, and when she did we both fell down under the power of God.

We had never seen or experienced anything like that in our lives. We're Missouri Lutherans and nobody goes down on the floor unless they trip on the rug and fall. So now, the Kansas lady is down on the floor and Frank and I are down on the floor, and I'm trying to get up. An usher comes by and helps me up, but Frank is still down, his whole body is shaking. Now I've known this man for many years and he doesn't do anything like that—never did. So I'm wondering what in the world is going on.

Then Miss Kuhlman said, "Oh, the glory on that husband." And I thought, *Here I am for months listening to you on the radio and you're going to talk to my husband and not talk to me?* "Oh, the glory on that husband," she said again. "Oh, the glory!" And she never laid hands on me. She never did really converse with either one of us. They picked up Frank and then she prayed a second time and we both went down again. They picked us up and then they took us off the platform. We never spoke to Miss Kuhlman at that meeting.

"GET UP!"

On the way back to our seats, all of a sudden I looked over and saw my friend Shirley in the wheelchair. I said, "Frank, look, there's Shirley, there's Shirley. Get up, Shirley, get up!" I was motioning to her to get up, to stand up. Then Miss Kuhlman turned around and called to Shirley, "Honey, yoo-hoo, you in the wheelchair, you can get up anytime you would like."

"No, I can't do it, I can't walk. I have multiple sclerosis. I've been in a wheelchair for fourteen years," Shirley responded in strained speech.

Miss Kuhlman urged Shirley, "No, you *can* get up and walk."

"No, no, I'll fall."

"No," Miss Kuhlman said again, "you won't fall."

Then Miss Kuhlman walked over to Shirley and took her by the hands, and Shirley got up out of the wheelchair—healed! And within an instant, Shirley ran back and forth at the front of that First Presbyterian Church in Pittsburgh, Pennsylvania. We were overwhelmed by this miracle! Shirley was healed—we were healed! Ironically, none of us ever spoke directly to Miss Kuhlman.

When the service was over, Frank picked up the wheelchair and we all walked to the car. He threw it in the trunk and we got in the car to head home. All the way home I kept saying, "We've got to come back and we have to bring everybody we know who needs healing—we've got to come back!" The entire way home I was writing down the names of all the people I knew who were sick. "We're going to go home and call them. We're going to get them here. We're going to take them to be healed!"

On the way to Pittsburgh, Shirley had to be spoon-fed baby food—but on the way home after she was healed, she wanted to eat a great big meal at a truck stop. We stopped at one and she ate a steak, baked potato, and a piece of lemon pie—and she ate it all.

AN UNEXPECTED REACTION

After eighteen hours on the road, we arrived home very early Saturday morning. We went first to Shirley's house and knocked on the door. Richard and their four children came to the door. Frank said, "I've got your wife." We opened the screen door and Shirley walked in. Richard just stood there, awestruck; and the kids just stood there, shocked. The children had never seen their mother standing up. They only saw her sitting in the wheelchair.

Shirley and I made a plan. The next day was Sunday and we planned that Shirley and I would arrive right before the church service started. We would walk down the aisle to the front pew and sit down. Nobody ever sat in the front row of our Lutheran church, nobody. They always sat in the back of the church, ready to get out after exactly one hour and not one minute longer.

So we arrived at the church Sunday morning, and Shirley and I were walking up the steps while Frank was parking the car. The church door opened and the pastor walked out and stood on the top step with Shirley's husband, Richard, and an elder of the church was also standing there. The pastor looked at me and said, "How dare you do this?"

Surprised, I said, "What...what...what are you saying? She's healed. Pastor, she can..."

He said again, "How dare you? You've taken her to a witch and this woman will die just like the doctor said she will, and you will die just like the doctor said you would."

By that time, Frank had parked the car and was on the steps and heard what the pastor said.

"Come on, Joan, let's go home," Frank said.

That pastor never backed off. He believed that what the doctor said was real.

Frank and I both said to the pastor, "God healed us. It's different. The doctors had nothing to do with it. They couldn't change it. They could not do anything about any of it."

That was fifty-one years ago. Since then, God has allowed us, as a family, to serve around the world and to spread the Gospel of Jesus Christ and tell hundreds of thousands of people our story of healing. And now there are many other miracle stories that have been added to our journey with our God, the Great Physician.

God completely and totally changed our lives. The last day I was in that church, the pastor said to me, "I don't want to hear you talk about this again, go to hell." And that was our invitation to leave. My great-grandfather was a charter member of that church and put the bricks in for the first building. My entire family was born, baptized, and confirmed in that church, but we left.

We still have had no contact with that community; most of the members of that church think that we're religious fanatics. Even so, I love them and I adore them. People there have been born and died and we've gone on our way, and now we have a family so big that we can't even count them—all over the world, all nationalities, all colors, all races.

Through one miracle, one touch of God's healing hand, everything about our lives instantly and dramatically changed. Yes, this transformation came with misunderstanding. It came with hurt, abandonment, and resistance from those who simply could not understand what had taken place. My thoughts? It was worth it all—a million times over!

Chapter 2

———•◆•———

WALKING IN MIRACLES

From the moment I received healing, it was my desire to take people who were ill to the miracle services where they could be miraculously healed. There were so many people who were sick—people who believed the pastors and the doctors who condemned them with a death sentence. We knew so many people in need of physical and spiritual healing.

So I told Frank, "I'm going to charter a bus." Within a day or two I chartered a bus. But then I had to cancel it because I first had to tell the people what we were doing!

It took us a couple of months to get our first bus filled with sick people from everywhere in St. Louis and even in the state of Illinois. We placed a brief advertisement on the radio that aired right after Miss Kuhlman's program. It stated that we were chartering a bus to Pittsburgh, Pennsylvania. I don't remember how much it cost. It was just a cheap little ad, but from that outreach we filled buses. All the years Miss Kuhlman was alive, we served her in that capacity. For the next eight and a half years, every month we took a bus to Pittsburgh, sometimes a couple of buses.

We expanded our outreach to include the other cities where Miss Kuhlman would hold healing services. We followed her wherever she went—chartering buses and even planes. We brought people from all across the United States of America to the services—and they returned home healed.

Frank and I love to talk about those exciting days, but we also talk about today because these days are as important as those days. Those days are past; they're history, but today the Spirit of God in our lives is even bigger. We've learned a lot over the years—He is always teaching those who want to learn. Now we have healing rooms in St. Louis. We preach and pray for people worldwide, and we had the honor of being part of Kathryn Kuhlman's ministry until the day Jesus took her home.

Don't feel like you need to charter a bus or a plane to bring God's healing touch to someone. The point of me sharing this story is this: I was touched by the healing presence of the Holy Spirit, and after receiving my miracle, I had to *feely give* what I had *freely received.* This is what Jesus instructed us to do. We've been given so much. As we've been given, so should we freely give. As you experience God's supernatural healing power—maybe by even reading through this book and its testimonies—I want you to know that you can *walk* in it. The power of God was never meant to simply be displayed during crusades, conferences, or meetings. You carry His power because you are filled with His Spirit.

IN THE BEGINNING

After a few months of chartering buses and taking people to and from Miss Kuhlman's healing services, I called her ministry office and said, "My name is Joan Gieson and I was healed in a meeting a couple of months ago. I'd like to charter a bus to bring people to Miss Kuhlman's future meetings. Do I have to register or anything with you?"

"Oh, thank you for calling. That's wonderful. We'll expect to see you here," was the response. There was no personal contact with Kathryn Kuhlman at all except that first time when Maggie walked Frank and I to the front of the church. Other than that encounter, there was no real connection with Miss Kuhlman. She prayed for Frank. He fell down under the power of God. I went down under the power of God, but there was no exchange between us: "Hello, I'm Joan Gieson, I'm Frank Gieson, and you're Miss Kuhlman. We're so glad to meet you!" None of that. We went back to our seats and after the service found Shirley and headed home.

So we started chartering buses, like many people did from all over the local areas and way beyond, and we would all wait outside all night long and praise the Lord through song. We sang worship songs and praise songs and old hymns. Oh, those were wonderful times. The more buses we took, the more people called and wanted to go with us to be healed.

I was consumed with people calling because now the word was out that healing had hit St. Louis. Not that it wasn't there before, but many of the people who went along came back saying, "I just got on a bus and went to the Kathryn Kuhlman ministry and God healed me! I can walk!" Or "I can see!" Or "My illness is gone!" For some typical examples of what happened at the services, people got up out of their wheelchairs and ran. People with terminal cancer were healed. A brain tumor was healed. A healed blind woman and a healed deaf woman returned home and started talking about God's miracle for them.

Now our phone starts ringing off the wall every day. We don't have time to do anything else. We can't do anything else but simply respond to those in need. We're in it. We're knee deep in God's healing work.

Eventually Miss Kuhlman noticed our involvement and one day asked me, "Where are you from?"

"I'm from St. Louis," I responded.

"You are? I'm from Missouri, too. I lived near Kansas City, in Concordia. I was born and raised there."

So now we've got a lot in common. She called us the two Missourian women, and for whatever reason she liked me and I loved her and honored her as a woman of God. After that conversation, she expected to see us at her services.

Then one bus turned into two buses, two buses turned into six...and so on.

One day Miss Kuhlman called, "I think I would like to come to St. Louis; could you help me get that organized? What kind of auditorium can we find? There's something called Kiel. Could you investigate that for us and see what it would cost and how we could do it?" Then she told me the dates she would like to be in St. Louis.

Frank and I went right down to the Kiel Auditorium and talked to the people. We rented the Kiel Opera House (now the Peabody Opera House). It only held about 4,000 people; when she came, it was so packed that people had to stand outside and around the building hoping to get in the building. We couldn't accommodate them all, so the services were held outside.

A HOLY ESSENCE

After coordinating that service, we got to know Miss Kuhlman even more, and I adored her. I came to know that she wore Shalimar perfume, and I had to have a bottle of Shalimar. I wanted to know her essence and the fragrance surrounding her. I loved the aroma—but it was really the fragrance of the Holy Spirit, not the perfume that was so prominent. Where that woman walked, light was all around.

Now I'm not saying that Miss Kuhlman was infallible. She was a human being who made mistakes and had struggles, just like all of us. She was alone most of her life and she had walked away from her family somewhat because she felt the call on her life to follow the Spirit of God.

Every Friday she had a miracle service, and every Friday I tried to be there with a bus or two or three—or a plane load of people seeking healing. They couldn't hold seats for us—it was always first come, first serve. So we waited in line all night. We didn't receive any special treatment, but we were her friends and she was our friend, and we communicated regularly back and forth. We did not do this on a daily basis because we honored her and didn't want to be a bother. We simply didn't want to walk in that kind of a position.

One time we invited Kathryn to St. Louis to meet the wealthiest woman in Missouri, involved with the Petra Light Company. This woman had asked me to cater a dinner for her, as we were in the catering business at this time in our lives. We felt that Miss Kuhlman's ministry could benefit financially, so we invited Miss Kuhlman in to meet this lady and we cooked the food for them. It was the best food we ever made and served—even though we walked out of the store with a little bitty brown bag full of $40 worth of food. At that time, $40 was a lot of money for one bag of groceries.

The wealthy woman listened to Miss Kuhlman—and that was it. There was never anything exchanged. So we realized that spreading God's Gospel wasn't in the hands of the wealthy; they weren't responsible, they don't always understand such a call. It's those who want to seek after the God who truly loves them and forgives them and wants to heal their bodies who will share the Good News. This was certainly the case with Kathryn Kuhlman. The motivation of her heart was to see lives touched and changed by the One she so dearly loved—the Holy Spirit. It's never about money—that's not the key.

The word *key* reminds me that we introduced Kathryn to the mayor of St. Louis, who presented her the key to the city. At a later date, she was also given the key to Pittsburgh, Pennsylvania for the positive influence she had on both cities.

LUNCH WITH MISS KUHLMAN

Kathryn Kuhlman was invited by special arrangement to visit and have lunch with a very wealthy woman who lived in a huge concrete castle surrounded with acres of botanical gardens—the largest in the entire city of St. Louis. Kathryn was impressed with the beauty of the gardens and with the furnishings within the home. Although we know wealth was not the key to a successful ministry, we hoped that the meeting between the two women would be mutually beneficial. As previously, this meeting was for naught. Kathryn simply left the estate and went to the healing service being held that evening.

At the service, Albert Firestone of the Firestone Petroleum business walked up to me and said, "Mrs. Gieson, I'm Albert Firestone and I'd like you to cater a party for me." Coincidently, he was the executor of the wealthy woman's son's estate. Her son was mentally unstable and being cared for in some kind of a nursing home on Long Island in New York.

I didn't know who he was and said, "Oh yes, fine. Listen, I'm very busy right now but look me up in the phone book and call me later." Two weeks later Albert Firestone called me and said, "I want to have a party for a special friend of mine." The special friend turned out to be the wealthy woman I mentioned earlier—and the party was exceptionally extravagant. He had food flown in from France and we served

Russian caviar and gourmet items of every kind. The party was attended by forty of the wealthiest people in the country. It was a very big deal!

Mr. Firestone had lived in Pennsylvania. He said he was the black sheep of the family and moved to St. Louis because the mountains in Missouri were like those in Pennsylvania. He bought a farm in Dutzow, Missouri and also had a house in the city of St. Louis. When back East, he lived at the Waldorf Astoria in New York City. This was a most unique ministry opportunity the Lord was opening up for Frank and me—hospitality ministry through catering. I am amazed to reflect back on this season and notice the very distinct fingerprints of God on every step in our journey.

After I was healed and we were spending so much time transporting people to Miss Kuhlman's events, the business Frank worked for disbanded. He had a sales job and it went out of business. We went for a year and a half without any income. Then one day when I was sitting at the table trying to figure out what I could feed my family that evening—because the cupboards were bare—God said to me, "Go into the catering business." I looked around and nobody heard Him but me. And I thought, *How do I do that?* A moment later it came to me to put an ad in the paper. For less than $4 I posted: "Catering—large and small—Joan's Catering."

USED BY GOD

With that word from God and that one lunch that we thought didn't yield any results, we enjoyed twenty-five years of owning a successful catering business, which was considered by many as the best—and we served the best. We did our best and we made money to support our family. We were booked up to a year and a half in advance, and the money we made from the catering business afforded us to continue to travel with Miss Kuhlman and pay for people to attend who couldn't afford the bus fare.

We also helped others charter buses to get people to the services where they received healing. We filled buses with people from all over the city, and any other city, who wanted to attend. And so it was our purpose in life to be used by God to provide access to Miss Kuhlman's healing services.

Could it be that, like Frank and I, God is setting you up for something absolutely wonderful? Don't look at what you are doing right now or what you have been given talents for as secondary and less spiritual than the man or woman ministering from the pulpit. We were able to have a unique role in the move of God because of catering. Yes, catering. Something that many people would have considered to be a "natural," not a spiritual occupation actually opened a supernatural door for us to have a major role in connecting people with the healing power of God. Ask the Lord how, what you're doing, right now, can help connect those around you with the love and power of Jesus. I promise you, these are prayers He delights in answering.

FUN MIRACLE STORIES ON THE ROAD

I've got to share some of the fun miracle stories that we saw take place on the road as we did the bus ministry. You will read many testimonies throughout this entire book, but I want to start listing some very unique ones.

For instance, there was Sister Mary Luke—a Catholic nun who would sneak in and out of the convent with our help. It was like a scene from an espionage movie where someone is kidnapped in the dark of night and taken off to the unknown. Well, with our friend the nun we would sneak behind the bushes and get into the car; then we'd whisk her off to get her on a bus headed for a Kathryn Kuhlman service.

Sometimes she would hitch a ride with us so she could visit a friend of hers in Columbus, Ohio. A few days later she would call and say, "Are you guys having a bus coming back from Pittsburgh?"

"Yes, Mary Luke."

"Well, can I get a ride with you? Pick me up in Columbus."

So there we are in a great big road bus driving down the highway and the driver says, "Look up there! There's your Catholic nun standing along the road in her black and white habit (nun's garment) holding a suitcase." What a sight! The bus would stop and pick her up and she'd get in. Then she would get out some little instrument she used to play, like a ukulele. We would all sing and have a good time.

One thing I learned very quickly is that healing had little to do with Kathryn Kuhlman. It's truly the work of our merciful and loving Jesus. Even though I have tremendous respect for this woman and am forever grateful, I got to have some part in God's plan unfolding through her, I saw time after time where people would receive divine healing without any involvement from a minister.

People would get healed coming and going from the crusades. There were many people healed before we ever got there—and it had nothing to do with me or anybody else, only our wonderful healing God. The people were expecting to be healed, and so God wasn't a respecter of places; He can heal anywhere when you're worshiping Him. When His healing presence comes into a building or into a bus, it doesn't matter—miracles start erupting! We saw the most outlandish healings; people with terminal cancer were healed. One time, Mr. and Mrs. Montgomery traveled with us and the lady, less than fifty years of age, was dying of cancer and was told she only had a few weeks left to live. We didn't even know if we should take responsibility for her on the bus. But God instantly healed that woman on the bus—and she felt it the minute it happened.

MIRACLES HAPPEN

Miracles abound wherever and whenever people believe. God shows no favoritism of place or time or person. He has no favorite denomination or expression of Christianity. That's just a matter of our own preference, the churches that we attend and how we worship, where we worship—but as long as our eyes are kept on Him and nothing else, everything is going to come out all right. He will change the night into day.

He will change the horror of death into the beauty of life. I've seen it and personally experienced it most of my life.

Since I was 27 years of age—we had our little girl, she was just a baby, and we had Michael who was four—we have followed the Spirit of the Lord without exception. We have penetrated places that we normally couldn't have, but not with talking—with living. If people can see Christ in you, they can believe Him in you. If just words come out of your mouth with no godly lifestyle to back up those words, they won't believe you. But when they see how you live and they see your kindness and love, they will believe. God does not show favoritism. He treats everyone with compassion. That's the way it was on the buses. When people boarded the bus, they could expect good things to happen; sooner or later it happened.

I tell people that we walk in miracles every day. What does it mean to walk in miracles? Well, as you walk forward into God's will for your life, God does whatever He wants to do to bring out your purpose. Out from each one of us the Spirit of God exudes; He lives; He's around us. We don't have to tell people we're Christians. I never tell anybody I'm a Christian. They can either know it and feel it and see it because they are open to God's Spirit, or they can ignore it and miss the greatest opportunity this life has to offer.

Many, many people had their physical and spiritual lives changed because of Miss Kuhlman's ministry. Some of the biggest churches in St. Louis were established and built with people who were brought into the family of God during a Kathryn Kuhlman service. And the buses, if you can imagine eight and a half years of hundreds of buses with thousands of people seeking and receiving healing—God is so good.

If people can see Christ in you,
they can believe Him in you.

A 17-year-old and his mother and father rode the bus to Pittsburgh to attend a service. On the way back to St. Louis the young man said, "How can people be healed like that? I'm going to be an evangelist. I'm going to go out and preach." He gave his heart to the Lord after that service. Today, Ron Tucker pastors Grace Church, one of the largest churches in St. Louis. So many lives were transformed by God's miraculous power during that wonderful season. And the most exciting thing was that it rarely ended with someone receiving a miracle and then going back to life as normal—if "normal" could even be an option after experiencing a touch of God. For so many, the miracle was a Heaven-sent gift calling them into their destiny. Destiny always begins, first and foremost, with knowing the One who knit us together in the womb. It begins with knowing the Lord Jesus Christ.

"THERE'S SOMETHING WRONG"

One time we had several buses going to Pittsburgh, and when the buses were almost filled, I said, "Frank, there's something wrong, there's something wrong. There's somebody on one of the buses that should not be going. I don't know why, but someone is going who's not supposed to be going on the bus." So we waited and waited for something more substantial to happen. Then, it was time to go. We had people to pick up over in Illinois at shopping centers, and then we'd head toward Pittsburgh.

With the buses all loaded and ready to pull out, a man called me at home. I wasn't going on this trip, and he said, "You know, I just can't make it this time." I thought, *That's probably the man who's not supposed to be going on the bus. Good, mystery solved.*

But then later, Frank called and told me that when the buses arrived in East St. Louis and people lined up to board the bus, out of nowhere a seven-foot-tall man, a big monstrous giant, approached. When he stepped up into the bus, everyone noticed because his body smelled so badly, an almost overpowering stench, an evil smell. Frank thought this was probably the man I was talking about. When he called and told me about the man, I said, "Frank, get everybody to pray for the bus—this is the man I told you was not supposed to be on the bus."

So Frank discreetly told the people to pray for that particular bus—still not sure why or what the problem was. Then all the buses took off down the highway. A while later, the caravan pulled into a gas station. Two guys were sitting there watching the traffic and killing time. When "monster man" walked out of the bus to go to the bathroom, the two guys were so scared they got up and ran behind the building.

I kept praying. When they finally arrived in Pittsburgh, my secretary, who is not even five feet tall, and another woman checked into the Carlton Hotel where everyone was staying. The Carlton is a really old hotel and here are two women staying in the room together and down the hall is this big man staying by himself. They called Frank and said, "We're going to go down and minister to the guy." So they walked down the semi-dark hallway and knocked on the door, went in, and ministered to the guy.

The two brave women found out that his alias was "Tiny" because of his size, and he was in the construction business in East St. Louis. He had just contracted with a killer to murder someone. That's why he was on the bus, to establish an alibi. In case it all went wrong, he had hand grenades strapped to himself to blow himself up if somebody found out about the whole thing.

Even after this tragic story unfolded, the two women ministered to the guy. Eventually he was saved, accepted Jesus as Lord, and ended up going to a monastery and becoming a monk. This all happened because he boarded a bus going to a Kathryn Kuhlman healing service. His life was completely changed. Although he wasn't "supposed" to be on the bus, God used our prayers to turn the situation around for our good—and His glory!

We didn't believe any of that stuff, but Tiny brought some newspaper articles that showed he was wanted by the FBI, the FCC, all kinds of people. He was a bad dude, but God took care of all of that.

Don't miss the power in Tiny's story. This man experienced a powerful, miracle turnaround in his life—not because he was going to a healing meeting. Quite the opposite! He was using our bus trip as an alibi, being motivated by murderous intentions. What happened? He didn't meet Kathryn Kuhlman—Tiny met Jesus through the two bold women who went and ministered to him in his hotel room. I am not advocating this approach for everyone, especially with women ministering to men. That's not the point. Use wisdom and discretion but, above all, step out in boldness.

There are so many different healing stories we have personally witnessed over the years. It's amazing—God is amazing.

We see miracles day after day because we simply step out and believe the Word of God. Believing is not measured by what you know; it's measured by what you *do* with what you know. James reminds us that faith without works—corresponding actions—is dead (see James 2:17). Faith saves you, no question. It's your belief in the saving work of Jesus that translates you from darkness to light (see Col. 1:13). Here is where we need to understand the connection between faith and works.

Kathryn Kuhlman was a simple woman from Concordia, Missouri, who decided to step out in faith. She moved. She acted. She took a step. She didn't live content just knowing about Jesus or knowing what He *could* do. She wanted to see God move, so she did what the Bible said. She did what was written because she wanted what was written in the pages of Scripture to be seen in the world around her. Don't you long for this? Don't you long to walk in miracles, like I wrote about earlier? There is no magic, special formula. God is looking for people who believe Him so much that they *act* like they believe. They act like Jesus heals. They act like God is a miracle-worker. They act and God acts. God is sovereign King. He doesn't need you and He doesn't need me. He doesn't *need* us or anything, but He chooses to use us. He chooses to work through us. Let's really believe that. Let's believe that the same God who worked through Kathryn Kuhlman wants to work through you!

———·◆·———

Chapter 3

THE LEGACY AND
IMPACT OF
KATHRYN KUHLMAN

In the following chapters, I am going to share some key principles that we gleaned by knowing Kathryn behind the scenes. Up until now, I wanted to share a little bit of my story, just so you know where I'm coming from and that I am not anyone specially qualified to walk in miracles. Jesus is the miracle worker, and the same Jesus who worked through Kathryn Kuhlman and Joan Gieson wants to work through you. I believe that with all my heart. My prayer is that the stories I shared, both from Miss Kuhlman's meetings and even some of the unique miracles that took place before and after the meetings, would stir your faith. May you walk away from reading this book declaring, like Kathryn did, *I believe in miracles because I believe in God.*

HER LEGACY: MY REFLECTIONS ON KATHRYN KUHLMAN, THE WOMAN

Although we weren't with Kathryn when she passed away in 1976 in Oklahoma, we knew she was sick. We received a call asking us to "Pray for Miss Kuhlman. She is sick and she's going to be okay, but just pray." We certainly did. Ours was the next scheduled service she was to have in St. Louis. We were all ready. We had the Kiel Auditorium already rented, anticipating 18,000 people. We had people already chartering buses that would be packed with people who were going to fill the auditorium.

As the night progressed, it wasn't OK and she passed away. We attended the memorial service, not the funeral. The memorial service was in Pittsburgh, Pennsylvania, and we also had a memorial service at a large Presbyterian church in St. Louis, which was filled to capacity. People from everywhere came to that one because so many were actively involved in her ministry.

Even today, years and years later, there is a void left by her passing. Kathryn Kuhlman was a simple Missourian woman who really wasn't into all the show. She wore conservative Ralph Lauren clothes on her very tall and thin frame. She almost always wore a straight skirt with a big white belt, a tailored shirt, and wedge shoes with straps around her ankles. She was very thin, not one ounce of fat, and she wore a big gold bracelet with diamonds on the front that was given to her by the owner of a shoe company. She was a fairly simple but classy woman—like 1,000 percent class. Everything she did was class.

Miss Kuhlman had an air about her; her presence was known no matter where she went. For example, Frank and I were at the Chase Park Plaza Hotel one day, sitting in the corner of the huge entry foyer full of people and noise. All of a sudden we heard someone walking in the door, way across the room, and it was Miss Kuhlman. Everybody stopped what they were doing and looked to see who it was. She had a captivating presence. The Spirit of God was with her all the time.

THE PRESENCE OF GOD RESTING UPON KATHRYN KUHLMAN

People were naturally attracted to Miss Kuhlman, and of course they wanted to be close to her. Because there are unsavory types in the world, after each service there were men assigned to usher her out quickly. Frank was one of the main guys who moved her safely from the platform to an exit.

There was another man who traveled with her all over the country, but when we were with her Frank was the one who helped her. These guys knew she was afraid of elevators and things like that, so they would seek out a safe place to take her after the service ended.

At this particular venue in St. Louis, the path they chose went directly into the kitchen. The whole wall behind the platform was wooden and the door was barely visible from where the audience was seated, but the guys knew where it was. So the second she said, "Amen," they escorted her off the platform, down the steps, and through the door to the kitchen.

As was my routine, I went up onto the platform to pick up all her things off the podium—her books, a little handkerchief, whatever she had left there. Then I went through the same door and into the kitchen. There I saw about twenty-five chefs with their tall white hats and white jackets and aprons. When I saw Miss Kuhlman pass by the chefs and wait staff, I heard all this clinging and clanging of pots and pans and whatever they were holding at the time they fell to the floor as the power of the Spirit touched them. Miss Kuhlman looked back and chuckled at the sight—amused at how the Lord used her to touch people. Kathryn had the greatest sense of humor. Her escorts then ushered her into the servant's elevator to go up to the floor where her room was located. All those people were struck down by the power of the Lord, and she said not one word nor touched one person. Now that's something I had never seen before and have never seen again.

STAY PREPARED

When Miss Kuhlman wanted to do something out of the ordinary, she had a bodyguard named Donnie, a bodybuilder, who accompanied her. Donnie would follow her around, moving people out of her way and keeping her safe. But she, too, knew how to get people to move. One time I was standing next to her in an auditorium and apparently I didn't respond to a move she wanted to make. So she came over to me, and on a really tender spot in my side, she discreetly but firmly squeezed that spot with her fingers and then twisted. You talk about moving, I had no choice!

One time we were in Minneapolis, Minnesota, and as Kathryn was tying up her shoes after changing her clothes, I went to get her a glass of orange juice and a newspaper, like I did after every service. There were always comments about her in the newspaper that we all wanted to read. So on the way back with the juice and paper, I heard a voice say, "Hey, Miss Kuhlman."

She said, "Yes, how can I help you?" while finishing working on her shoe.

Very disrespectfully, he said, "Hey, how long does it take you to get ready for a service like that?" I was shocked—shocked that this guy got into the room and shocked at his tone.

But rather than being ruffled as I was, she looked at him and said coolly yet politely, "Oh sir, I really don't think about it. I just stay prepared." A profound statement that's been with me for more than fifty years. "I really don't think about that. I just stay prepared." That's how we Christians should always stay—prepared.

Kathryn didn't live with a "ministry face" that she took on and off during the appropriate times. Her life *was* the ministry. She didn't view herself, or any piece of her life, as separate from God. We see God's original plan for this in the Garden of Eden where He spent His days walking side by side with Adam and Eve. Before sin, they did not know life apart from walking with God's presence. Kathryn fully embodied God's original plan by walking alongside Him all the days of her life. Because of this, she never had to strive for the Holy Spirit to come because He was already there. If a sick person was presented unexpectedly, she was prepared to pray on their behalf for a miracle because God was standing beside her.

We were created to live prepared. Peter and John are the perfect example of two men who were stopped unexpectedly and still allowed God to move through them.

> *Now Peter and John went up together to the temple at the hour of prayer, the ninth hour. And a certain man lame from his mother's womb was carried, whom they laid daily at the gate of the temple which is called Beautiful, to ask alms from those who entered the temple; who, seeing Peter and John about to go into the temple, asked for alms. And fixing his eyes on him, with John, Peter said, "Look at us." So he gave them his*

attention, expecting to receive something from them. Then Peter said, "Silver and gold I do not have, but what I do have I give you: In the name of Jesus Christ of Nazareth, rise up and walk." And he took him by the right hand and lifted him up, and immediately his feet and ankle bones received strength. So he, leaping up, stood and walked and entered the temple with them—walking, leaping, and praising God (Acts 3:1–8).

Perhaps if Peter and John did not align themselves with the Holy Spirit daily, that man could have lived the remainder of his life crippled and in pain. The same goes for Kathryn. If she did not live her life in reverence and submission to His presence, hundreds if not thousands of people would have lived their lives in pain and without an encounter from the Father. This is an important lesson to learn because we see that surrendering our lives does not only benefit us but also the lives of many we encounter. Sometimes, we are the only chance for an encounter from God that people could have.

Not long ago, Frank picked me up at the airport. He was waiting for me right out front, so I jumped in the car with my luggage in my hand and we left, traveling to the office. A few blocks from the office, I noticed a man park and get out of his car. He started walking around the car and then fell down on the ground. Frank didn't see what happened.

I said, "Frank, stop! A guy just got out of that car and he fell on the ground. Turn around, Frank." So Frank turned around and there was the man lying on the ground. He had no pulse, no breath. I told someone who came by and stopped to call 911. I started to pray over this guy and ask God to bring him back, to let him live. Then the ambulance came and the guy—who I thought to be dead—opened his eyes, stood up, and then laid down on the stretcher.

I don't say that to brag; I simply relay that story because we have no idea what we will face from one minute to the next minute. We have no idea what God is going to present to us. But as men and women of God, there is nothing impossible for those who trust the Lord. So we lay hands on the sick and expect them to recover. We speak the words of freedom to those who are captive. We don't have to tell anybody we're Christians. We live it out and we stay prepared, knowing that it's God's great joy to work through His children.

A HEART FOR OTHERS

Kathryn often gave away things at Christmas time. She didn't have a big party; rather, she gave money and toys to orphanages and places where there were groups of children. She sent gifts to children in other countries and also sent them locally. Not many knew what she did for children at Christmas. I never knew that until I was working in her office. Miss Kuhlman had a very generous heart. In fact, not only was her spiritual heart largely compassionate, her physical heart was enlarged as well and was what eventually took her home to Heaven. She passed into eternity during open heart surgery.

Another important insight into her character was one time after a service when I saw her sitting at the end of the counter at a nearby soda fountain store. She was just sitting there, so I slowly walked up to her because I didn't want to startle her. She looked over at me and said, "Joan, Joan, why weren't they all healed? Why weren't they all healed, Joan?" That's it. "Joan, why weren't they *all* healed?" That was a question that she went to the grave with. Perhaps she was thinking, *What should I have done? How should I have done it? Could I have done it better?* There was no pride in her. That wasn't the situation at all. But her striving in life was to do better, to become more like her Savior.

Kathryn didn't become a minister for her own personal gain. In fact, she often did not even like to read what others were saying about her because she never wanted to buy into the hype. Her life and her love was Jesus, and she devoted herself to seeing Him be given the glory.

Many times when someone is given such a large platform, it is easy for their hearts to fall into pride. However, Kathryn never saw her anointing as anything other than the Holy Spirit working through her. Her heart for others was shown through her generosity, which she never asked for recognition for. It goes without saying that many people were healed, but Kathryn didn't want to be praised or recognized for those. She simply cried out to God asking why *everyone* wasn't healed. She didn't allow the healings to boost her ego; rather, her heart broke for those who left without receiving their miracle.

Perhaps the reason Kathryn was so successful in her ministry is because she never stopped searching for more. While she celebrated the miracles, she questioned the ones that didn't come to pass. While she never allowed that to deter her faith, she used it to bring her closer to God. She asked Him the hard questions and never stopped pursuing His heart.

THE OFFICE

Miss Kuhlman's office in Pittsburgh was in an older building filled with older furniture. It was a very quaint, simple operation. A couple of secretaries here and there and then she took us over. She said, "Come here, I'll show you my office." There was a rounded bay window on the corner of the building, the kind they used to have in the old days. There were about five windows around the whole thing, and next to the window was a great big, old-time wooden desk with a big microphone sitting on it. It was an antique microphone that they had back in radio days, and that's what she used to record her radio program. We have a whole lot of tapes of Kathryn Kuhlman's programs. I taped every one of the programs daily; and when we listen to them now, we can hear the traffic outside in Pittsburgh. Sometimes, she would even open the window and talk to the policemen outside. She knew all the policemen. She'd wave and open the window and talk with them about anything and everything.

On the other side of her desk was a rug. It was just a small, worn oriental rug. She would lie on the floor every day on that rug and talk to the Lord. I guess it was her serious time when she didn't have an answer and she was really searching for an answer. It had been there so long that her silhouette was pressed into that rug. It had been with her through all the years—unique yet simple, nothing extravagant or special, no silver or gold thread. She was plain but elegant, absolute class to the nth degree.

Both Jesus and Kathryn made it their priority to be able to get away and spend time with the Father. This relationship then fueled their lives, which created a space for the Holy Spirit to move through them to bring healing to others.

FULL-TIME CHRISTIAN

Kathryn Kuhlman gave herself entirely to the work of Jesus. She was not a part-time Christian. She didn't do one thing one day and another thing another day. She did not live her life in compartments, where Christianity was just one part of the bigger whole. The Lord was her everything. She was the same person on the platform as she was behind closed doors in the office. Her mind, spirit, body, and everything, her every breath was to serve God. She was totally yielded to Him, and out of that came total surrender. From that state of mind and spirit, God used her to heal—even by walking past people He wanted to touch through her.

Kathryn lived her life with excellence. She considered herself a "full-time Christian." Hebrews 4:13 says, "And there is no creature hidden from His sight, but all things are naked and open to the eyes of Him to whom we must give account." Kathryn lived her life, both public and private, openly before the Lord. Her life was her sacrifice of worship. Because of this, the Lord granted His favor upon her and her ministry. People came to her meetings knowing that it was a safe place because of the relationship with God that she had cultivated.

People have said to me that there are those who are anointed by God, and when they come out from behind the podium on the platform, everything changes. When they pass by, there's something supernatural that happens; and I understand that because I served a person like that. She was not in it for the money or the fame. She was not using Christian ministry as a way to get her name "out in lights." She was compelled by a sense of divine destiny to ultimately see people meet the love of her life, Jesus.

You know, there's not one thing in my home that I've bought. Everything has been given to us. We pay $3,000 a month for our house. There's not an offering that ever comes in. All we deal with is homeless people and sick people and they haven't anything, so only God provides for us. I don't even know how it comes. The point is, it's not about things for us and it was never about things for Kathryn Kuhlman. She was yielded. She was yielded, totally given out, totally sold out. There are few men and women today who walk consistently in that mindset or lifestyle. They have agendas. And I'm not saying bad things. All of us have to earn livings. I have to earn a living. I don't know how I do it, but it happens. I have a roof over my head and food in my belly and I am grateful. Don't misunderstand what I'm trying to say here. Having things—material possessions—is not bad. Earning a living is not bad. Working is not bad. Walking in the financial provision of God is a blessing, not a curse. The problem with many today is that they are driven by self-seeking agendas rather than the simple burden to see the broken made whole. It's not about introducing people to Joan Gieson or Kathryn Kuhlman—it's about introducing them to Jesus because He is the only One who can do anything about their situation.

Miss Kuhlman was so given to the Lord that where she was, God was, and where she walked,

He walked, and why wouldn't it be that way? It's like your shadow. You cannot dislodge your shadow from your body. Your shadow is there. I'm not saying the Spirit of God is the shadow, not at all. He walked *in* her. She was yielded to Him in everything. She didn't take what she wanted and reject what she didn't want.

Kathryn lived a life of excellence. This is most likely due to the fact that she walked hand in hand with the Holy Spirit. She never allowed her relationship with God to take the back seat to her ministry. She lived in constant communion and communication with the Father. Because of this, her faith was always strong and expectant. Her lifestyle was similar to that of Jesus. He spent His days in communion with God, which gave Him the faith to be able to leave His quiet space and allow the Father to work miracles through Him. Luke says:

> *Now it came to pass in those days that He went out to the mountain to pray, and continued all night in prayer to God. … And He came down with them and stood on a level place with a crowd of His disciples and a great multitude of people from all Judea and Jerusalem, and from the seacoast of Tyre and Sidon, who came to hear Him and be healed of their diseases,*

as well as those who were tormented with
unclean spirits. And they were healed. And
the whole multitude sought to touch Him,
for power went out from Him and healed
them all (Luke 6:12,17-19).

She never claimed perfection. She never claimed to be something on her own. Some people would see her as Kathryn Kuhlman and think, *Well, she's a spiritual superstar; she's closer to God than I can ever be.*

People have mistakenly insinuated that I act like Kathryn. On the contrary, I don't try or want to act like Kathryn Kuhlman. I don't have any thought in my mind to act like Kathryn Kuhlman. Do I want to be like her? No. I want to be the best Christian Joan Gieson can be— the best person God created me to be. I strive after His Spirit. I don't try to elevate myself or emulate anybody else.

This is the invitation of the Lord for you. He doesn't want you to emulate me or Kathryn Kuhlman or any other notable figure. Most certainly, you are interested in Miss Kuhlman's ministry and legacy if you are reading this book. And rightly so! I admire her. I honor her. I deeply and dearly respect her. It's OK to honor someone. However, let's not confuse honor with emulation. In our honor for someone, like Miss Kuhlman, let's allow their lives to speak to us as wonderful invitations.

THE ASSIGNMENT OF THE ANOINTING

If God could make someone like Kathryn Kuhlman so unique, working specially through her gifts, talents, and personality, the same God wants to work through you. When the anointing rests upon you, everything comes to life. It's like black and white going into full color. Before we know Jesus, all of this potential is living inside of us, just waiting for the touch of His presence.

Friend, know this—there is healing in His presence. Yes, physical healing for every disease and malady, but also healing to every place and person who has been afflicted with darkness. The anointing of the Holy Spirit, the very presence of God *within you*, has been given to you for a purpose. God's anointing comes with God's assignment. What is the assignment of God's anointing? Jesus made it very clear when He introduced His ministry to the world:

> *The Spirit of the Lord is upon Me, because He has anointed Me to preach the gospel to the poor; He has sent Me to heal the broken-hearted, to proclaim liberty to the captives*

*and recovery of sight to the blind, to set at
liberty those who are oppressed; to proclaim
the acceptable year of the Lord* (Luke
4:18-19).

What has the Spirit of the Lord anointed you
to do? *To preach* and *to heal*. If anything could
be said about Kathryn Kuhlman, she completed
this task. She was faithful to fulfill the assignment of the anointing—to preach and to bring
healing. Understand that this is your assignment too! This is not just for Kathryn Kuhlman
or Joan Gieson or any other "healing minister"
you can bring to mind. You are a healing minister. You are called to administer God's healing
touch here on earth to the people around you.
May the examples in this book remind you of
this wonderful assignment, not reserved for
the exclusive few but made widely available to
whosoever will.

I've worked with two of the most influential
evangelists of our time—Kathryn Kuhlman and
Benny Hinn—and they called *me*. I didn't call
them. Sounds exciting, I know. I still have to
remind myself that this is the life that God has
so graciously called Frank and me into. Yet there
was nothing that uniquely qualified me for this.

Please know, I'm a simple wife with a little education, no money in the bank, and a house not even paid for. I wish to God my house was paid for, but it isn't and I've lived there 45 years and it still isn't paid for. I drive a car with 300,000 miles on it. It's just a vehicle to use. It's just a house to have a roof over our heads.

I remind you of what the apostle Paul wrote to the Corinthians:

> *But God hath chosen the foolish things of the world to confound the wise; and God hath chosen the weak things of the world to confound the things which are mighty* (1 Corinthians 1:27 KJV).

God is looking for willing vessels. He's seeking those who will step past convenience and walk in bold love, faith, and trust. This is what it looks like to *walk* in miracles—a consistent lifestyle that is defined by love, compassion, faith, and trust. There's no reason to complicate it any more than that. God takes ordinary men and women—businessmen, housewives, doctors, lawyers, bankers, educators, store clerks, grocery store baggers—and He gives them an extraordinary gift. This is the gift of His anointing, His indwelling presence.

If we're born again, we have this indwelling presence of God available to us. He's living inside us! There is no closer that He could come and no greater level of power that He could supply you with. When you received the Holy Spirit, you received God. Period. This sounds thrilling, but so many children of God are not experiencing His fullness. They're not walking in miracles. Why the disconnect? After all, every Christian has been given the gift of the Holy Spirit. You have the same Holy Spirit that I have, that Kathryn Kuhlman had, that Paul the apostle had, and, yes, even Jesus Himself had. We have the same presence of God living in each of us.

The real question is, what we are *doing* with His presence?

Part Two

––•••––

UNTOLD SECRETS OF
Kathryn Kuhlman's
Miracle Ministry
AND RELATIONSHIP
WITH HOLY SPIRIT

Don't let the title fool you—by no means is this list comprehensive. This is certainly not *everything* I learned from Miss Kuhlman, but it does represent a collection of some of the most important and most transferable principles I learned from watching her, both on the platform and behind closed doors.

—•◆•—

Chapter 4

CREATING THE ATMOSPHERE

SET THE SPIRITUAL ATMOSPHERE

The atmosphere at each of Miss Kuhlman's meetings was everything. From the moment anyone walked into the church or auditorium or even the area outside where the service was being held, every person knew they were walking away from the world and into a spiritual place. Everyone felt the change in the atmosphere. It felt like even the air was different. It was like seeing with different eyes—spiritual eyes.

What helped create that exceptional atmosphere was the ministry's *reputation* and the people's *expectations*. It's important to identify these two key factors, because many people would assume that the atmosphere was set by the location, building, venue, music, or other aesthetic elements. Many churches have all of these items today, and so much more than was available to Miss Kuhlman, and yet there is a lack in the miracle-working power of God. I believe an atmosphere for the miraculous was created through reputation and expectation.

Kathryn carried an expectation for God to intervene and for miracles to take place. Her faith radiated off of her, which in turn shifted the atmosphere of every room she was in. People came with *expectation* to be healed.

The excellent reputation of the Kathryn Kuhlman ministry and the healings that happened in the services was the basis for the atmosphere that surrounded the people. There was a high level of integrity associated with her name.

People would travel for hours, even days to attend one of Miss Kuhlman's services. People who came were in pain, lost in their suffering, crying for help—people who were dying. They knew others had been healed; they knew this woman was being used by God to bring wholeness back into their physical bodies and restore their spirits. The reputation of integrity was what brought them, what gave them hope.

I believe an atmosphere for the miracles was created through reputation and expectation.

From the very first time we attended a service, we felt that special atmosphere that was created out of the commitment Kathryn had for being used by God. As Frank and I stood all night in front of the church and Shirley was in her wheelchair, we expected a miracle—and we weren't disappointed. We were three among a hundred, then three among a thousand, then thousands waiting with expectation. Bodies were leaning against each other, holding each other up for hours. Then someone started to sing and we all joined in—so many different voices combining into one glorious praise to God for what He was going to do.

REPUTATION, INTEGRITY, AND EXPECTATION

Reputation is what produced expectation. The reputation of Miss Kuhlman's ministry, and the testimonies of healing that resulted from her services, created expectation in the hearts of those who traveled from great distances to attend her meetings. They came, believing that the same healing God who powerfully touched those they heard about would also touch them.

Because of the reputation and integrity that was associated with Kathryn Kuhlman's ministry, people came with an expectation of being healed. That mindset was contagious and quickly permeated throughout the crowd. They knew what they were going to see and experience was real. Of course there were charlatans cashing in on the spoils—there always are. But Miss Kuhlman always kept above that, beyond reproach.

It seems that the reputation of Christians isn't like it used to be. There have been too many Christians, especially well-known ministry leaders, who have fallen, made mistakes that became national news. Or maybe it's the recklessness of life today. Many people don't follow real guidelines and don't have real guidelines for their children. It's like life is abstract today, and it's all there for the taking—whether you're five years or fifty years of age—what's in it for me. It's not like growing into life. Youngsters act like teenagers and teens act like adults. There seems to be no maturing along the way.

It used to be that parents led their children, guided them, and raised them with honor and respect for themselves and others; there's very little of that today. For example, most older people need help opening the large, heavy doors at stores, the post office, and the like, but it's hard today to find a young person who will hold the door open or help them out of the car. Unfortunately, there may be a reason for that. Maybe they're afraid they would get accused of hurting the person. Today is not like yesterday—and we're probably never going to see that type of societal environment again.

Taking that thought a step further, I can't even imagine the liability issues today of taking half-dead people halfway across the country in a bus to go get healed. If they died or something happened, there would be lawsuits filed immediately.

THE BUS RIDES: MIRACLES ON THE GO

Now, I want to step back from Miss Kuhlman's ministry for a moment and show you how you can create an atmosphere for the miracles in your life. That's the goal of this section of the book—I want to show you how transferable these principles are. This book wouldn't be complete if I didn't share the amazing story about Leslie.

They called at the last minute and we only had a couple of seats left on our bus. Eight-year-old Leslie had been in the hospital and her mother had heard from someone there about a "miracle bus" going to Pittsburgh, Pennsylvania (to Miss Kuhlman's meetings). Leslie's parents wanted their daughter healed from cancer. That's all we knew. Leslie was just released from the hospital, and her daddy carried her in his arms. He boarded the bus and gently lowered her onto the seat. We were all surprised to see the age of the child and to see how very weak she was.

During the long bus ride, Leslie and another passenger—a goofy guy in a natural, kind way—became friends. He was sitting across the aisle from her and every so often she would lean way over and tap him when she saw him sleeping. He would pretend to wake up startled and she would think that was so funny. They played back and forth; it was so cute.

Then in the middle of the night, while everyone was still wide awake, as her daddy sat beside her, she looked up at him and said, "Daddy, it's your birthday and Jesus is going to heal me. And I'm going to come back and that will be your birthday present because I don't have money to buy you anything."

Well, everyone on bus just fell apart with compassion for this darling little girl and the faith she had to be healed. For the remainder of the bus ride all the people were concentrating on Leslie. Many of us prayed. Every thought, every eye, every ounce of strength we had was focused on that little girl. She went like a trooper all the way, even though in pain. I am overjoyed to tell you that in that service God healed Leslie.

This was a genuine demonstration of the supernatural power of God. Truly, you could not fake or manufacture this level of miracle. Before Leslie was healed, her mother uncovered Leslie's cancer-eaten leg from the knee to the ankle, exposing her little leg that was completely split open to the bone from the cancer and all the radiation. The skin on her radiated leg was like black leather, it was burned so badly. The pain had to be excruciating for that little girl.

Right in the middle of the Kathryn Kuhlman service, God was healing Leslie. Miss Kuhlman stopped what she was saying and looked over toward where Leslie and her parents were sitting. "What's going on down there?" asked Miss Kuhlman. A doctor from Johns Hopkins Hospital was there and he examined Leslie's leg and said, "Miss Kuhlman, I can't believe it, but I see skin growing."

Hallelujah! The well-respected physician from a world-renowned medical facility saw that right down to this little girl's bone there was flesh growing and skin growing over the flesh. The doctor was watching and screaming—he had never experienced anything like what God was doing in that moment.

The ride home from that service was more than any of us could imagine. We were all in awe of God's miracle-working power to heal. We heard that a few days later, Leslie was riding her bicycle—healed and whole. That's a miracle!

Even though many would like to focus on what happened at Miss Kuhlman's meeting, I want to point out that we collectively created an atmosphere on that bus that fueled Leslie's faith to receive healing. Granted, she came into the bus with unusual faith! Still, our objective was to sustain an atmosphere that would keep her level of faith high. I encourage you to do the same. Meditate on the good works of the Lord! Think about His countless promises, boldly recorded in both Old and New Testaments, revealing His heart to heal. Get lost in the words and works of our Savior Jesus, who *"went around doing good and healing all who were under the power of the devil, because God was with him"* (Acts 10:38 NIV). Don't wait to arrive at the miracle service or crusade—create an atmosphere through your own life that keeps faith high. This is what we saw in bus ride after bus ride. The bus was no more special than the buildings where Miss Kuhlman held her miracle services. What made the bus a special place were the people who created an atmosphere for the miraculous!

ONE OF THE GREATEST MIRACLES KATHRYN EVER SAW

It goes without saying that our kids didn't have normal childhoods. When they were old enough, we would assign them to different buses so they could help the people who needed assistance— on the way to the Kathryn Kuhlman services. One son, who was 13 years of age at the time, remembers vividly carrying men off the bus to help them go to the bathroom on the long trip to Pittsburgh or wherever. He actually helped them empty their catheters and that kind of assistance. He said that he could feel the lifeless flesh on their dead bones—and smell death. But hallelujah! After receiving healing at the service, these same men left their wheelchairs behind and spryly walked to the bus, jaunted up the steps, and praised God all the way home for His mercy.

And then there was Bill Spears and the three "Jesus Freaks." Bill Spears was in the Army and was badly injured in the war. A doctor declared he was 300 percent disabled. Everything was wrong with him. One day he was lying on his bed, which was near the window, and three young people who loved the Lord, Jesus Freaks, walked by his house and said, "Hey Bill, we're going to go to a miracle service; do you want to come with us and get healed?"

"No, I don't want to go," he said.

But the trio wouldn't take no for an answer. They kept trying to persuade him and finally he said yes, but only because he wanted to get out of the house to smoke. They had to strap him into a wheelchair because his body constantly shook, and off they went to board the bus. After arriving at the auditorium, Bill was pushed over to the wheelchair section where he kept bumping into other wheelchairs because he couldn't control the throttle correctly. He was making a lot of commotion—with 16,000 people watching. He had a big catheter hanging out from under a big old lap blanket. And he was wearing the weirdest looking pajama bottoms and tops you ever wanted to see.

He was still making noise when Miss Kuhlman started the service. All was going fine until all of a sudden in the auditorium there was a very loud electrical explosion—like a transformer hit with lightning. Throughout the Kiel Auditorium there was a huge, loud moaning sound. We could feel it on our skin.

Frank and I were up on the platform with Kathryn—we were on either side of her. She turned to me and said, "Joan, find the noise. Find the noise. Find the noise." I pointed to Frank and said, "Find the noise." Kathryn couldn't stand noise. She actually leaned over and held on to the piano because she felt the noise within herself, as we all did.

We both left the platform and walked outside the auditorium through the doors. Then we reentered the auditorium through the doors where we could see the front of the stage and the backs of the audience. As we entered, it felt like a magnet was pulling us right toward this one particular wheelchair. Our bodies were actually being forcefully pulled. We came to a stop in front of a psychedelic-looking guy in PJs who was held down in his wheelchair with strong nylon straps; there was a heavy metal tray at his waist. The Jesus Freaks were standing next to him, and 16,000 people were staring at him.

Then all of a sudden the man stood up out of the wheelchair and the metal tray clattered to the concrete floor, the noise reverberating throughout the entire auditorium. The man's straps ripped apart—they didn't come loose at the hook. The straps—heavy nylon straps that usually take a machete to cut through—were ripped apart and fell away along with the lap blanket as he stood up. He staggered as he started walking down the aisle in his pajamas, with his catheter following him. Then the catheter came out and he started running—the catheter draining on the floor behind him.

By the time he reached the stage, the entire auditorium was totally silent. Miss Kuhlman was leaning on the piano and Frank and I were leaning on each other. We all expected the man to go up on the stage but he stopped. He turned around and ran back toward us. At his wheelchair, he took out the battery—he wouldn't be needing his chair ever again—and carried it to the front where he set it down, then jumped over it onto the stage, four feet above.

There he stood, healthy and healed, with Miss Kuhlman who was speechless. Little did she know that Bill Spears had epilepsy, multiples sclerosis, was blind and suffered from grand mal seizures, and more than a dozen other diseases and ailments. Unknown was the fact that he took twenty-seven different kinds of medication just to make it through each day. But God knew—and He healed Bill.

Looking at Kathryn, he said, "Miss Kuhlman, God has healed me." She was stunned, as were all the people watching the supernatural spectacle. In fact, near the time of her passing, she told us and others that out of all of the years she was in ministry, the healing in St. Louis of Bill Spears was the greatest miracle service she ever had. We believe that even right now the Spirit of God is still on St. Louis. We found out later that evangelists went to the city and prophesied that there would be a revival that would spark and spread.

I want to pick up this story in a moment. For right now, I want to go back to the beginning of Bill's miracle story and point out the "Jesus Freaks" who were responsible for bringing Bill to his miracle. Truly, this reminds me of the account in Mark 2 where you had a group of friends bringing their paralyzed friend into an atmosphere where healing was present. Jesus was there, which meant healing was there. This group who brought Bill Spears to Miss Kuhlman's meeting reminds us that we are on assignment to bring people into the healing presence of Jesus.

WHAT HAPPENS IN VEGAS...

At the end of the service in St. Louis, Miss Kuhlman said to 16,000 people, "Everybody, I want you to call Frank and Joan Gieson and make an appointment with them. Everybody is invited to come to our next service that is in Las Vegas. They're going to bring Bill Spears with them and he will be in Las Vegas with me." She wanted the witnesses with her.

Well, after this mega-service and all that happened, Frank and I just wanted to go home and go to bed. For a week, we wanted to hibernate like bears—and then she announced to this huge crowd to call us?! We didn't even get home before the phone started ringing; almost everyone wanted to go along. We had so many buses it was unbelievable. We also had to charter a large plane and a private plane to accommodate all the people.

I called TWA to charter the plane. Some of the seats were already reserved on that flight by businessmen who were in the back of the plane; we had the rest of the plane. At one point, a few of the men, who were tipsy from drinking, came up to us and one asked, "What's going on up here? Is this a family reunion? Who are you? What are you doing?"

Well, that's all it took for the group of us to talk about Jesus and tell them about His healing power and the gift of salvation. The businessmen were saved on the way to Las Vegas—how miraculous! Once again, this is a reminder that you carry the healing atmosphere of the presence of God *wherever* you go.

But nobody knows the trouble we went through from the day we left the auditorium in St. Louis until the day everyone boarded buses and planes headed for Las Vegas. It is unheard of to call hotels—any hotel in Las Vegas—within less than a week to reserve one room let alone hundreds. Everything is booked up months in advance.

But God was listening to us and out of the clear blue sky someone called from the Marina Hotel, a brand new hotel, so new the construction material was still there and all of the decorating wasn't completed yet. No one had ever stayed there before. Only the finest from God.

The healing service in Las Vegas was amazing in so many ways. Many, many people were healed and Bill Spears gave his testimony. His story was witnessed by such a large crowd that there was no denying God's miracle. From that service, hundreds told hundreds more about the saving grace of the Lord. Surely generations were touched and continue to be touched with how Miss Kuhlman allowed herself to be used by her heavenly Father.

CREATING ATMOSPHERES OF FAITH

Bill's miracle was one among multitudes of reports that gave reputation to what the Lord was doing through Kathryn Kuhlman. Did everyone accept or believe these accounts? No. Miracles do not guarantee salvation. More often than not, yes, the demonstration of signs, wonders, and miracles is attractive to unbelievers. This is why we must preach and demonstrate the Gospel, heeding the words of the apostle Paul:

> *And I, brethren, when I came to you, did not come with excellence of speech or of wisdom declaring to you the testimony of God. For I determined not to know anything among*

you except Jesus Christ and Him crucified.
I was with you in weakness, in fear, and
in much trembling. And my speech and my
preaching were not with persuasive words
of human wisdom, but in demonstration
of the Spirit and of power, that your faith
should not be in the wisdom of men but in
the power of God (1 Corinthians 2:1-5).

Miracles give evidence to the fact that Jesus is alive. He is real! He is powerful! Nothing is impossible for Him. There will always be those who reject testimonies of the miracles simply because their hearts are not open or receptive to the reality of Jesus. That is a very real response people have to talk of miracles: "I don't believe *that.*" My own pastor in the Lutheran church had a very negative response to the miraculous.

Yet I believe there are many more people who are desperate to hear miracle reports. Why? When we start reporting or sharing about the miracles we have seen Jesus do—or have personally experienced in our own lives—it creates faith in those who are listening to us. They think to themselves, "If Jesus can do it for them, He can do it for me." This is what I saw happen so many times with Kathryn's ministry. Reports got out of what mighty things God was doing in those meetings, and those reports created expectation. Expectation drove the sick, hurting, and broken to Miss Kuhlman's meeting. I'd say that expectation created an atmosphere of faith in those meetings.

Kathryn carried a child-like faith that so many of us struggle to have. In Matthew 18:2-3, Jesus says, "Then Jesus called a little child to Him, set him in the midst of them, and said, 'Assuredly, I say to you, unless you are converted and become as little children, you will by no means enter the kingdom of heaven.'"

Kathryn never doubted whether or not God was going to move. She believed, and He did! She truly had an essence about her where you couldn't help but believe in miracles if you were around her. She knew that the miracles were not dependent on her own abilities but on God's. Because of this belief, she was able to overlook self-doubt and look fully into the promises of healing from Jesus.

Likewise, you can create an atmosphere of faith by sharing about the wonderful works you've seen Jesus do—on your behalf or maybe for someone else. Share about the mighty deeds of the Lord and, just as it was with Miss Kuhlman, those stories will create an expectation in the people around you!

Secret #1
CREATE ATMOSPHERES
FOR THE MIRACULOUS

It was through reputation and expectation that Kathryn Kuhlman created atmospheres of faith for miracles to happen in her meetings.

1. **Reputation**: constantly speak about the *reputation* of Jesus by sharing about the miraculous works He is doing in and through you.

2. **Expectation:** as you share testimonies and stories of miracles, these will build faith in the people around you. They will begin to believe that the same God who performed a miracle for you or through you can do the same for them.

————•◦•————

Chapter 5

My Best Friend: Intimacy with Holy Spirit

We heard Miss Kuhlman consistently say, "Holy Spirit is my best friend." Her relationship with the Holy Spirit was like being closer than a wife is with her husband and vice versa. When you're married a long time like Frank and I have been, sometimes Frank does not have to say a word to me and I know exactly what he's saying to me. That's how it was between Kathryn and the Holy Spirit.

For another example, as a rule I know exactly what Frank's going to order on the menu. I know everything about him. I know him from the top of his head to the soles of his feet. I know how he walks. I know what pants he's going to wear with what shirt. That's an earthly, human explanation of a close relationship; but when you walk with God's Spirit, you become one, and when you yield to Him, nothing comes before that. You are constantly and totally in tune with Him.

I'm not saying that Kathryn Kuhlman was perfect; no, there were mistakes in her life because she was a human being. But spiritually she was married to Him, she was dedicated to Him, her life was in His hands. She trusted Him fully— enough to stand up on the platform in front of thousands and say, "Someone there in the third row has a tumor on your eye and God is taking that off right now. Stand up, please. Stand up. Where are you? Where are you?"

And in the third row a woman would stand up, "Here I am, Miss Kuhlman, here I am." And the woman's family would be crying and sobbing because that's exactly what happened—her tumor was gone. Miss Kuhlman came from the other end of the world and this woman came from this end; they had never seen one another, never talked to one another, and we knew it because they were from our own buses. There was no knowledge or thought of this woman with the tumor prior to that moment when Kathryn declared from the stage that cancer was being destroyed.

Miss Kuhlman walked with His Spirit. She knew Him. He knew her, and He knew He could trust her. God's Holy Spirit could trust her to execute what He had to tell her—and she wasn't afraid, she wasn't ashamed. There was no part of her ashamed. There was no part of her afraid to do His bidding.

In today's culture, it has become easy to settle for a relationship with the Lord that is close to non existent. Many go to church, sing a few worship songs, and then go about the rest of their week without really pursuing the Lord any further. We've settled for the bare minimum, yet when it comes to our relationships with people we are much more intentional.

Marriage is a beautiful example of how our relationship with God should look. In fact, God goes as far as calling the Church His Bride! God's desire is to be in relationship and communion with us with the closeness of a husband and wife.

Ephesians 5:25-27 says, "Husbands, love your wives, just as Christ also loved the church and gave Himself for her, that He might sanctify and cleanse her with the washing of water by the word, that He might present her to Himself a glorious church, not having spot or wrinkle or any such thing, but that she should be holy and without blemish."

Kathryn knew the importance of stewarding her relationship with God and not treating Him as some fictitious character but as an actual person. The story of her oriental rug speaks volumes to her devotion to the Lord. She spent so much time on that rug in prayer and in God's presence that the rug had a permanent imprint of her body. Wow! She knew that nothing of worth would be brought forth in her life if she did not steward her relationship with the Holy Spirit! She treated Him as her husband. She allowed herself to be fully seen before Him. It was noted that she had the type of relationship with God where she could easily just sense what He was doing without having to ask. We see another example of this relationship with the Father in Jesus' life. John 5:19 says, "Then Jesus answered and said to them, 'Most assuredly, I say to you, the Son can do nothing of Himself, but what He sees the Father do; for whatever He does, the Son also does in like manner.'"

Neither of them performed miracles for their own glory. The miracles were just an overflow of what was already inside of them.

PART-TIME AND FULL-TIME CHRISTIANS

I mentioned our son earlier—how he helped the men on the bus on the way to services—and there is another story about him that I want to share. He and our other children attended Christian schools. We wanted them to learn about the Lord as well as academics. Well, one time Mike had to take off two days of school because we asked him to be in charge of thirteen buses. At that time, he was in his first year of high school and 15 years of age.

It was his responsibility to count the people and pretty much keep track of each one such as who could walk and could not, who needed bathroom help, who did not. He had a list we gave him, but he was in charge of looking after the people on the list. We trusted him with that, and he would accomplish his tasks with excellence.

This particular time, the services were Thursday and Friday, and when Mike went back to school on Monday, the teacher said, "Michael's back and we're glad to see him."

Then the teacher asked, "Who in this room believes in miracles?" He was the only one who raised his hand—even though the school was Christian, supposedly instilling godly values and beliefs.

At this Christian school, he was ridiculed and made fun of until we finally took him out and enrolled him in a public school. The environment, sorry to say, was better in the public school than it was in the Christian school.

But before that all took place, when Mike was in kindergarten, I met Anne Richards— and she changed my life for all eternity. He was born with allergies and suffered with them for years, as well as bouts of pneumonia. I had read in the Word of God, the Bible, "Is anyone among you sick? Let him call for the elders of the church" (James 5:14). So I went to an elder of the church where I attended all my life. Mr. Richards, Anne's husband, was an elder of the church, although I didn't know him personally until that time. I called the elders of the church and asked them to pray for Mike. Nothing happened that day and I was disappointed.

A few weeks later, Mike got sick at school and I was supposed to pick him up. I was too sick myself at that time and couldn't drive. Anne Richards volunteered to get Mike and bring him home. She stopped first and picked me up and she drove to the school. After getting Mike settled in the car for the ride home, Anne started talking to me about a personal relationship with Jesus. I was surprised by her perspective and I listened to every word she said. As she witnessed to me, I realized there was so much I was missing in my life. I met Jesus that day, and she became our spiritual teacher and so much more for many years, for all of us—our entire family.

After listening to Kathryn Kuhlman on the radio for a few months, I called Anne and told her, "Anne, I'm going to go to her healing service." She said, "Okay." I was healed and have been healed ever since, and that's all these years later. But we have given our lives to the Lord to serve Him regardless what it takes, regardless what physical and financial troubles we have. I'm not saying ministries can't be rich, though we never did get there. But we're the richest people in the whole wide world because we follow Him. I'm learning every day. I learn from the homeless people who come in every day to be fed. There's something new. There's something different. But I know the power of God because I've walked in it. I've seen it. It's happened.

HOLY SPIRIT'S PRESENCE

Kathryn Kuhlman was one of the strongest human beings I ever met in my life—not in stature but spiritually. When she sat down, she was so tall and thin it was like folding up an accordion. You could put her in a shoebox, but the strength and the aura around her of God's Spirit was so enormous that people would fall like leaves from trees around her. Like the time when she walked through that restaurant kitchen, and the pots and pans and lids and spoons fell along with the chefs and staff. I watched her then as she turned around laughed at the demonstration of the Holy Spirit's power. It was funny to her to see that happen because she didn't really understand it either. She really didn't understand what or why it happened, but I could see it. Although we couldn't actually see the Holy Spirit, we could see her and the effects of the Holy Spirit's presence in her.

Kathryn carried such a strong presence of the Holy Spirit that unsuspecting people would sometimes fall over from the weight of the presence that followed her. We see a similar story through the life of Peter. Acts 5:14-15 says, "And believers were increasingly added to the Lord, multitudes of both men and women, so that they brought the sick out into the streets and laid them on beds and couches, that at least the shadow of Peter passing by might fall on some of them." This leads us to believe that just by being under the shadow of Peter, people received their healing!

I'll never forget that time I saw Miss Kuhlman walk through the kitchen. I did not see the Holy Spirit, but I saw the evidence of the Holy Spirit. She walked in the Word, not being afraid, not appeasing everyone in the congregation whether a politician or someone of great wealth was present. She spoke clearly, encouraging all to accept Jesus Christ as Lord and Savior. If you follow the Word of God, all things are possible. Although Heinz (of Heinz ketchup) was one of her supporters, she never allowed her integrity to be compromised for personal financial gain.

Today, too many evangelists and pastors have sold themselves out to appeal to those who have money and can get them into higher places. We live in a day when money is very important and prestige is sometimes even more important.

A LITTLE GIRL'S HUMBLE SPIRIT

Miss Kuhlman was humble. She never bragged. She was never a braggadocio. And as mentioned previously, the clothes she wore were beautiful and elegant but simple, not flamboyant. One time when we were in the office, she wanted to show us something and we were ready to follow when all of a sudden Maggie, her main secretary, came toward us pointing to her watch and saying, "Miss Kuhlman, Miss Kuhlman," like she was trying to protect her from us taking up too much of her time. "Miss Kuhlman, don't forget you have that thing to take care of."

Kathryn said, "Oh, don't worry about that, Maggie. Joan and I, we're going to have some fun. Come on, Joan." And she just took off like a little girl. "Come on, Joan. Come on in here."

We followed her down the hall, and she showed us a large wall made of old-time dark mahogany sliding doors. As she slid open one door after another, from the top to the bottom was filled with audio tapes of all her radio programs. She said, "These are for posterity." Wow, we were really impressed at the historical value.

Then she said, "Oh, come here, come on," and she took off again. "Let me show you my office kitchen. This is how we cook around here," Kathryn said. She walked over to the oven and opened the oven door—it was full of papers! Although much business life took place in that office, she took time to be funny. She wanted to have fun; she was like a little girl in some ways. Today she had her friend Joan over and she wanted to have some fun with her, just kind of fool around. Dealing with sickness and life and death almost daily, it was no wonder that she enjoyed levity from time to time, and I enjoyed being part of it.

She had a large straw hat with a scarf wrapped around it and tied around her neck—like Katherine Hepburn wore. Sometimes Miss Kuhlman, even in her later years, would put on her hat and big sunglasses and drive her convertible with the top down. She zoomed in and out of traffic; she was a pretty spiffy old lady. She got around, met people, never met a stranger. Her father was a simple man in Concordia, Missouri; so was her grandfather. There are stories she wrote about that time in her life; others have written about those times as well.

FORESHADOW

Concordia, Missouri is the headquarters for the Missouri Synod Lutheran Church

Organization, and the parent organization of the church we attended. One year, two people from the Walther League (a Christian youth group focused on Scripture and fellowship) were selected to represent our church at the convention, which was in Concordia, Missouri. I was picked as a representative and I was thrilled. This was long before I knew Kathryn Kuhlman or had any kind of personal relationship with Jesus. Yet I feel as though this experience was an example of God giving me a foreshadowing of things to come!

The church paid our way on a bus, and in Concordia it was arranged that we would stay with a Lutheran family there. I was in one home and the other girl who went with me was in another home. It was so much fun. The first thing we did was go to the football game of the Concordia Seminary. There was a big bonfire and I was with lots of people who were having fun, but I felt all alone. I remember the loneliness I felt. This was the first time I was away from my mom and dad; I was 13 years of age. I decided to walk away from the bonfire at the school, the Concordia Lutheran Seminary. I walked away by myself and stopped at a Methodist church. I sat on the church steps and cried and cried. I didn't know why I was crying, but I remember crying. Then

I walked some more and stopped at a house; it was a big house. I sat at that house for a while and I could hear all the screaming and the fun that the kids were having at the football field.

I remember walking from there to a drugstore on the main drag. The drugstore was closed and there I sat; then the people I stayed with came looking for me and found me and said, "Joan, what are you doing here? Why did you walk away? We lost you! We were worried about you." I really didn't have an answer for them. So we went back to their house.

I found out much, much later that when I walked to that Methodist church and I sat on that step, that was the church where Kathryn Kuhlman had her salvation experience. I had no idea at the time—didn't even know who Miss Kuhlman was. And the house steps that I sat on—that was the house where Kathryn Kuhlman was raised. And the little drugstore, the kind that had food and candy, was where Kathryn Kuhlman visited frequently. By that time, Kathryn Kuhlman had moved away from Concordia, Missouri.

I visited all those places and had no idea that I would one day be part of Kathryn Kuhlman's ministry. Every life has a purpose, and somehow God put me in that position. Now, was there an anointing from that? God connects people in life to accomplish His plan. There I was in Concordia running around on my own—why would I go sit on church steps and cry?

Even though I was a church kid, never missed a Sunday, I still wasn't spiritually alert. I had not accepted Jesus Christ as my Lord and Savior, didn't even know there was such a thing. I knew about Jesus in the major ways. I knew He died on the cross. I knew that He went to Heaven, but I didn't know of anything personal. I knew the stories, the second week of Epiphany, the third week in Advent, I knew all of that; but I didn't know anything at all about Jesus except the children's stories. Until He became my Lord and Savior, I was lost; but God had a plan and He put me right in every place and time where I could eventually fulfill His purpose.

That belief of mine is confirmed in the rest of the Concordia story. When it was time to return home from our time in Concordia, I missed the bus. The family came looking for me, again. "Where were you, Joan? You missed the bus." It just so happened that the bus turned over and people got hurt and some were killed.

I'll never forget that Concordia trip. I was different. My purpose for being there was other than the barbeque, the wiener roast, the bonfire, and all that. That was normal kid stuff, but I was somewhere else. I was about my Father's business, and didn't know it. I had no clue that those places where I sat, a woman prior to me sat on those same places and gave her heart to God and was serving God. I had no idea Kathryn Kuhlman was alive on the face of the earth. I didn't know anything about that, but God knew from the beginning. It's been a really neat journey with Him through life.

WHAT SET KATHRYN KUHLMAN APART

Again, I find it necessary to mention that I am not writing these words to try to exalt a person. Rather, I want you to see why Kathryn Kuhlman enjoyed the level of relationship with God that she did. Miss Kuhlman was distinct, not because of anything she had but because who she gave full control of her life over to. She made an unwavering decision to be friends with the Holy Spirit. Perhaps this was one of the greatest examples I got to witness while spending time in her presence. You see, I was able to spend time in the presence of someone who was under the influence of His presence. It was her friendship with the Holy Spirit that positioned her to walk in miracles. Likewise, it's your closeness with the Holy Spirit that gives you the ability to experience a lifestyle of miracles. There is no formula. You cannot turn friendship into a formula or set of rules, otherwise it switches from friendship to religion.

Secret #2
CULTIVATE A LIFESTYLE OF INTIMACY AND FRIENDSHIP WITH HOLY SPIRIT

Kathryn Kuhlman did not pursue formulas on how to walk in miracles—miracles followed her because miracles follow the presence of the Holy Spirit. When your ambition in life is to cultivate intimate friendship with the Spirit of God, you become saturated in His presence. And it's His presence that releases healing.

Chapter 6

---•◦•◦•---

I'm Not a
Faith Healer

It's All about Jesus

Kathryn Kuhlman did not like to be called
or labeled a faith healer. She did not like that
at all. Her ministry was about God the Healer,
not her. As stated previously several times, she
was humble and genuine. Well, she was also a
rascal as a kid. She wasn't perfect and she made
her share of mistakes along the way. Maybe
that's why she didn't want to be called a faith
healer—she wouldn't presume to have more
faith than another.

Now I can't say for Kathryn Kuhlman, but her ministry saw healings because she allowed herself to be used by God—whenever and wherever He chose. Being an instrument of His came later in life. As a kid, she was a bit of a scoundrel, a wiry little girl. We talked to the people who owned and operated the drugstore, and they remembered Kathryn as a fiery little red-headed kid—and the apple of her daddy's eye. She could do no wrong. Even her mom took second place to Kathryn with her dad.

She wasn't a sit down, keep your mouth shut, don't do anything wrong little girl. She was always in a little trouble here and there. I don't mean legal trouble or anything like that, but if mom said turn right, she'd turn left. Why were these early footsteps shaped like that? God has a purpose and a plan and a timing. There is a time to groom and train a horse until it becomes a winner.

God grooms us all of our lives, and if we yield to Him, He uses us. Miss Kuhlman yielded her life. She was a little stubborn at first and had a little problem. She married the wrong man, divorced him, and lived a life alone. She was alone. She didn't do things that most single women do. She dedicated and gave herself to the Lord.

In obedience to God, she slept in a lot of barns as she traveled around Missouri, Illinois, and the Midwest. There were many, many years of sleeping from place to place while preaching His Word. She admired her predecessor Aimee Semple McPherson's wildness, tempered by the Holy Spirit.

Kathryn never claimed to be a "faith healer." Her real, main emphasis was Jesus. That's who and that's where she wanted to lead every person in every service. She wanted all to know about God's Spirit. She wanted people to rely on Him. She wanted everyone to pray in the name of Jesus and know that it was Jesus who did it all—all the healing, all the forgiving, all the sacrificing. She would never take one ounce of credit because she knew who she was. She knew she could screw up. She knew she was fallible and human.

She could be your friend. She was somebody you would want to eat lunch with, somebody you would have wanted to talk to, somebody you would want to sit next to in a restaurant and just chat. She was appealing like that. She was never standoffish. She didn't like titles. She didn't like labels because the Holy Spirit was so far beyond her. It was all God. "He's God and I'm just serving Him," was her mantra. And she didn't like the accolades. She didn't like the lifting up of herself in any way. I think she was partially concerned about that, too, for fear that she'd believe her own press. She never wanted to buy into that.

Kathryn never claimed to be a "faith healer." Her real, main emphasis was Jesus.

Miss Kuhlman had a stuttering problem when she was young, and she went and studied how to correct it. The way she spoke was why some people made fun of her. She was so dramatic when she talked. She actually wanted to make sure she said it correctly and clearly.

God gives each person a mind and He knits each body together in our mother's womb. We have a body, a soul, and a mind, but we're not aware of our spirit that's around us all the time. The day we are born again we have the spirit of God, but until our mind understands what it's all about we can't appreciate what we have. I believe that when Kathryn Kuhlman dedicated herself to what God wanted her to do, her spirit kept growing around her. That's why when she walked anywhere, others could feel the Spirit of God on her.

EVERYTHING IS POSSIBLE

Perhaps the reason Kathryn saw so many miracles was because she was so deeply aware that the miracle worker was not her; it was Jesus. With this in mind, she didn't think anything was impossible. If Kathryn Kuhlman observed herself as a miracle worker, there would be limitations. Human beings can only go so far in their limited ability and power. This was not Kathryn's perspective. She rejected the label of "faith healer" because she *knew* that she was not the healer. Everything was possible because God was limitless. Everything was within reach because God lived inside every true believer. So the miraculous was an everyday occurrence to her—yet she was always delighted and awestruck by His faithfulness in every service.

Kathryn was so completely simple that anyone could stand in her presence and not feel intimidated by what she knew or who she was. She was an everyday human being living with the living Spirit of God inside her—and she never thought there was anything impossible. She had a childlike understanding and childlike belief that she could walk into the darkest places and shine God's light. That lifestyle and mindset is contagious. If you're around someone who lives like that, you become like that because you understand those beliefs. Your motions go in those directions, believing that nothing is impossible.

I think of some of the things that God has allowed us to do that were absolutely supernatural. For example, God gave us the provisions to feed 34,000 people at a dinner, even though we had nothing, but only a few days prior. People would laugh us out of town if they didn't believe in the grace and mercy of a heavenly Father. God also provided those people with a week's worth of groceries for the whole family. God is good; His faithfulness endures.

It's not what you have. It's what you don't have that you can believe for. It's not what is already right there, obvious. I can't go to the bank and have them give me enough money to take care of me for the rest of my life. I have to trust Him every second of every day. It's a challenge, but it's also a great opportunity to give Him all the glory because only He can do that. Could it be that God is calling you into such a lifestyle of faith? It demands eyes that are fixed on a

limitless Jesus. If I were to focus on the impos-
sibilities stacked against me and used those as
the basis for whether or not I would have faith,
I'd *never* put faith to work and never see the
miracles. I encourage you, take your eyes off
yourself—what you can do and what you can't
do—and put your eyes completely on Jesus.

When Kathryn Kuhlman would walk into any
auditorium, you could hear a pin drop. There
could be 50,000 people present, and yet it would
be so quiet that you could hear a pin drop. If
somebody would go "Shhh," you could hear it.
It would reverberate throughout the whole auditorium. That was how much respect people had
for Miss Kuhlman and for the atmosphere that
was filled with the Spirit of God. People came
expecting a miracle, and they got it. She had
nothing to do with it. She was the first one to
say, "I have nothing to do with it, nothing."

SIMPLY YIELDED

Why didn't Kathryn want to be described as
a faith healer? Because she knew herself. She
knew the Kathryn Kuhlman who was a little
redheaded rascal. She knew the Kathryn Kuhlman who had a funny sense of humor and could
make snide little comments. She knew the real

Kathryn Kuhlman was not God. She knew she could not heal herself. She couldn't heal her friend. She couldn't heal anybody; only God could. In yielded simplicity, she was able to walk. In that total yieldedness she was able to be amazed that God could use His little freckled redhead, that God could do something with this little girl. Everything amazed her. She was delighted and delightful.

She was grateful for everything that came to her, and she started taking care of Korean and Chinese children. She would send money and things and it amazed her that she could do that. She was buying dolls made in China—and sending them to China for the children. Very few people knew, or even know now, how much Kathryn Kuhlman gave to the poor and how generous she was with her resources for the poor.

———◦———

Why didn't Kathryn want to be described as a faith healer? Because she knew herself.

———◦———

Even fewer people know that Miss Kuhlman organized a men's choir made up of healed alcoholics. Many of these men were drunk out on the street, and then they would hear the music and the singing and want to learn more about Jesus. Or she'd pass by them and say, "Good morning," and they would follow her and get saved. The whole choir was made up of men who were once overtaken by addiction; then they accepted Jesus and put on their white suits and white ties and sang praises to the Lord.

A lady named Mrs. Ivy Boyer was on my first bus. Ivy was a widow who had a little bit of money. Her husband had just passed and she was sick—she was dying. She heard about the bus and called me about it, but she said she was too sick to go. I said, "Mrs. Boyer, get on that bus and go. God will heal you." Sure enough, God healed her and she lived for years after that. Although she gave everything away, she lived a rich, full life as a healthy woman.

JESUS IN YOU

Remember this: God leads each one of us in a different way, and if we follow Him, even though it sounds crazy, God will take you on an adventure that you will never ever forget. I can attest to this firsthand. God has had us on a wonderful journey ever since I received Jesus as my Lord and Savior. It has filled our lives with great joy, meaning, and purpose. Is life without difficulties? Of course not. We face trials and circumstances just like everyone else. In fact, those who walk in miracles tend to experience suffering on a greater level than most, in the same way that Jesus often confronted the depths of human suffering. In order to bring healing, we need to recognize the needs of the people. These should stir us. They should provoke us. We should burn with a desire to meet those needs, *not* through any power or solution we can bring—we are powerless! I am powerless! However, the One who lives inside of us has *all* power. No disease can stand against the Spirit of the Risen Savior within you. It's not you against sickness, disease, and devils—it's Jesus *in* you, just as the apostle Paul described: *"Christ in you, the hope of glory"* (see Col. 1:27).

Remember this, dear reader. Apart from the indwelling presence of Jesus, you can do nothing. This is why Kathryn Kuhlman so staunchly rejected the label of being called a "faith healer." The problem with that description is not necessarily the "faith" part—it's a human being considered a *healer.* There is one Healer and His Name is Jesus. Kathryn knew herself and she knew her God, and she never got the two confused. She lived mindful of her shortcomings—one of the greatest was her inability to bring healing to anyone. Jesus was the Healer. The power of the Holy Spirit, released in Jesus' Name, was what released healing.

Allow this same wonderful Holy Spirit to flow through you! Remember, it's *Jesus in you*. Live mindful of this truth, just as Kathryn did, and I believe that is one of the ultimate keys to walking in miracles.

———————•◆•———————

Secret #3
LIVE AWARE THAT JESUS IN YOU PERFORMS THE MIRACLES

Kathryn Kuhlman rejected being called a "faith healer" because she recognized that human beings cannot release divine healing—only God can! Let this bring great relief to you, as it takes all the pressure off of you trying to manufacture the miracles. Remember, it is absolutely impossible for you to perform any kind of miracle; it is Jesus in you who works the miracles. Live mindful of this glorious truth. Apart from Jesus, you can do nothing, but working in partnership and cooperation with Jesus *nothing is impossible!*

————————●——————————

Chapter 7

COMPASSION UNLOCKS THE MIRACULOUS

Time after time Jesus was compassionately moved by the people in need. But I think sometimes people almost want a formula for moving in miracles without really having a revelation of compassion. Miss Kuhlman was a compassionate person. Everyone could see in her attitude and feel in the atmosphere of the services the genuine compassion she had for those present.

There is a definite sense of a real caring, a real love in someone who is sincerely compassionate.

There is a difference between someone "sweet talking" you and someone who is authentic. Compassion is an absolute. Without compassion, nothing good will happen. An evangelist can demand that a guy walk who is having a problem walking, and the guy may walk a bit, but the guy is never healed. Only the compassion of the Spirit of God heals people, and only the evangelist who has the compassion of God's Holy Spirit can see the results of what he or she has been set on this earth to see. The person being used by God will see the people who received miracles walk out of the service. The same person will see, ten years down the road, people come back and say, "I was in your service ten years ago and now I have my own business. My legs are working; my spine was healed that day." Praise God!

Only those kinds of things can you see from a man or a woman with real compassion. It's not about money. It's not about position. It's not about name-dropping. It's not about any of that. It's yielding to God's will and purpose. Compassion is life-giving. Compassion changes life and lives, and is contagious. You can experience it. You can understand it. It's a visual thing in your spirit. You can see it. You can feel it.

  Only the compassion of the Spirit of God heals people.

WHY WEREN'T THEY ALL HEALED?

When I saw Miss Kuhlman in the pharmacy in Minnesota that day with her head in her hands, that revealed to me her compassion—a heart that ached for those who weren't healed.

She was lamenting, "Why didn't they all get healed?" She wasn't bragging or gloating about what a great service it was. Even though the church was packed out and we received more than $100,000 in donations, none of that mattered to her. None of that was important.

It was interesting that no collections were taken at Presbyterian churches. I don't ever remember her asking for donations. Yet the funds came in. God was involved in every aspect of those services—no matter where they were being held.

There were some in the ministry whom Miss Kuhlman loved and invested her time and prayers into. One young man was such—she adored him; he was the child she never had. He served the ministry well and did a lot for the ministry, but he in some way wasn't fully committed to it or the Lord or something. It seemed he always had to learn and go a different way and do things differently—there was no consistency in his walk, in his journey with God.

> *Walking in the Spirit of God means that there is no separation. It means that the person is sold out totally and there is no separation between God and His child.*

Now Kathryn Kuhlman, she walked in the Spirit of God; she walked in that always. I'm reminded how Sid Roth asked me, "What does that mean—walking in the Spirit of God?" And I told him and many others that walking in the Spirit of God means that there is no separation. It means that the person is sold out totally and there is no separation between God and His child. It doesn't mean that the person is God—not anything like that—but the totally committed person and God are one, and that includes His Holy Spirit. So if you are totally committed to God, you think like Him, you act like Him, your first thought when people gather is, *What can I give to you? Do you need water, can I give you food? I want to comfort you. I want to feed you. I want to take care of you. I want to take care of whatever is on your heart. Why are you sad? Let's talk about this. Let's change it.* That's the Spirit of God inside when you do that, when you're always extending yourself. Nothing is too difficult. There's a song about that, isn't there?

NOTHING IS IMPOSSIBLE

Totally committed people have a nothing-is-impossible mindset, which reminds me of the time we were planning a Christmas dinner for hundreds of families. God told me to pick up the phone book and He would show me who to call and that's exactly what I did. I asked a guy at a dairy farm for 30,000 eight-ounce glasses of milk, and I asked him for at least 15,000 to 20,000 gallons of milk for families to take home. I also wanted dessert for the Christmas dinner so I also asked him for a mixture of sherbet and ice cream.

"Lady, are you nuts?!"

"No."

"Ma'am, you must be nuts. You're not even one of my customers. We're not supplying you with anything."

"I haven't just picked up the phone book and started calling people. God has you, sir, on His mind and I'm calling about providing a Christmas dinner for families in need. Please write down my name and phone number."

The guy was angry and didn't understand. He hung up the phone—and we waited.

About an hour later, he called back and said, "You know what, I don't know why I'm calling you back, but you get a truck over here right away, a refrigerated truck…and I'll give whatever."

Somebody had just pulled up to our facility a refrigerated tractor trailer truck, and it was exactly what his specifications were, so off went Frank and another guy across Illinois. When we crossed a set of railroad tracks, Frank almost flew out of the truck.

As Frank pulled into the dairy farm, they were getting ready to close. But the guy I talked to on the phone yelled out, "Back it over right there at the corner." He backed over to the corner and all of a sudden on a huge conveyor belt came carton after carton after carton after carton of milk—and cream and butter.

When almost finished loading, the guy asked Frank, "Hey, ain't you got something to hold all that stuff down with? You're going to spill the milk all over the place!"

"No," said Frank, "I didn't think about that. I just got the truck."

He said, "Hold on a second. I'll call over to my friend across the way." He calls his friend and says, "Hey, I got this dumb cluck over here with this truck and he needs something to hold his load down with. You got something?"

His friend asks, "What are you doing?"

He said, "I'm giving them milk. They got a Christmas party."

The other guy says, "Hey, I want to get in on this deal, too." So he brings us a whole load of ice cream to add to the load. And toys! This big ice cream business was giving away promotional toys for every gallon of ice cream, so they gave us toys too. Every kid at the Christmas dinner got a toy from that company—every kid.

We have no doubt that all involved behind the scenes with that Christmas family dinner were rewarded in many ways for the compassion they showed for people they would never meet.

ON THE ROAD AGAIN

Another time Frank was on the road, he was in a 30-foot motor home taking twenty-eight people to a service in Pittsburgh. A dozen lawn chairs were strapped to the top and the people stuffed inside were feeling like sardines. Pittsburgh is pretty mountainous and he had to drive up a steep hill to get to the Holiday Inn where everybody went in and booked a room for the night. Frank stayed in the motor home and enjoyed the nice sight from atop the hill.

When we all woke up the next morning, there was snow on the ground. Frank was very nervous about driving a big vehicle filled with people down a steep hill and across the river to Pittsburgh to get to church.

We made it OK but the streets were so narrow that he couldn't park on the street so he backed the motor home into an alleyway and we sat there looking at the church, waiting for the doors to open. Pretty soon the police came and asked, "What are you doing back here?"

"We're waiting for the church to open."

"Oh, okay," he said. We were relieved not to have to move from where we were tucked away.

But then we saw a garbage truck—and the dumpster was behind the motor home. Yup, we had to move. Frank pulled into a parking lot near a donut shop and we all bought donuts and coffee and sat there having a great time together. When it was close to the time of the service, Frank pulled the bus out and he had to drive around and around in circles because of the one-way streets. Then we saw a long line of big road buses dropping people off in front of the church. Frank pulled in behind them, hoping the police officer would allow him to drop our passengers off too. He did. But then had to drive the motor home way back across the river to park and hail a cab to get back to the church.

That story is special to us because not only did our passengers get healed in the service, just as many were healed coming and going while on the bus! We were never surprised at where and how the Lord chose to bring healing to the people who were expecting a compassionate Father's touch.

MERRIMENT AND MEMORIES

One time there was a little old man who was a retired engineer. He had had a heart attack and still had a bad heart, so his wife put him on our bus and he sat next to Sister Mary Luke, the nun you read about in a previous chapter. Not long into the trip, Sister Mary Luke pulled out her music stand and started playing her ukulele. She also played a mouth harp, which is something like a harmonica. She provided the music and everyone sang to the Lord. The retired engineer turned the music sheet pages for her. After that first bus ride, he booked himself every time the nun was on—he had to go and turn her sheets of music. After all, his heart was healed and he was so very grateful to God for the time he spent on the bus and at the service.

LEGACY AFTER LEGACY

Frank and I were talking just recently about how many of today's churches in the St. Louis area and beyond were actually started as the result of an experience on one of our Kathryn Kuhlman ministry buses. Three young men quickly came to mind. They traveled to a service with us and then went on to become pastors of very large congregations. Each started leading a small prayer group in their homes.

For example, when Ron Tucker (mentioned previously) was 17, he accepted Jesus as his Savior and consequently his church at the time threw him out because they said he had become a radical. Well, his mom and dad left too, and they started a little fellowship in their house, with just a few people. As the fellowship grew and grew, they moved to larger and larger facilities. Now Pastor Tucker leads a congregation of thousands. Ron Tucker was filled with the Holy Ghost on our first bus. Praise God!

Jeff Perry has a very similar remarkable story. He now leads the St. Louis Family Church in

Chesterfield, Missouri. God uses people who have compassion and a heart for others. God can use anybody willing to commit to God's will and purpose for their lives. You don't need a big certificate from a university. You don't need this or that gift. I can't sing. I can't preach. But God has used this little family of ours in miraculous ways!

FOLLOWING THE SPIRIT OF GOD

In those days, we took a whole bunch of people to Kathryn Kuhlman services. Basically, we tried to go every place she went.

But we did not follow Kathryn Kuhlman. We followed the Spirit of God. It had nothing to do with that lady, although she was very special in God's family. We, along with countless others in those days, were hungry for a real move of God's Spirit and Miss Kuhlman was one who truly modeled a vessel yielded to the Holy Spirit. This goes to show you that there are always people looking for a real move of God. Don't deny the people around you the very thing their hearts are crying out for. Don't wait for a move of God to break out in a local church—*you* rise up and be the move of God. When you move, God moves. How does God move? He is moved by compassion, as we see exemplified in Jesus. When you follow the Holy Spirit's movement, you are basically following a God who is moved by compassion. Find people and places where compassion needs to be released and I promise you, you're being set up to see some wonderful miracles released!

This is what I remember about those days traveling to Miss Kuhlman's meetings—we followed the Spirit and watched as God moved so compassionately, healing the sick and restoring the broken.

Our kids were practically raised in the backseat of a bus or a church or auditorium. We hired a teacher who tutored them in the back row. Nobody else could sit in those seats; they were reserved for our children and their teacher.

During one season, we followed the Spirit of God to Florida. Miss Kuhlman was scheduled to stop in a variety of different cities. We gathered a group of people and chartered a plane to fly down to Florida. We rented cars and started off on the west coast with services in Tampa and Ft. Myers, then we drove down to Miami. We went to Orlando and then to Jacksonville.

Jimmy McDonald was the African American singer who sang with the ministry. We were good friends with him—he was an amazing vocalist. He sang at a Good Friday service for me one time. Between scheduled healing services, we decided to visit a church that Jimmy McDonald had in Florida. He had an AME church in Kansas City too. So we made a point to go to his church on the following Sunday—which happened to be Jimmy's birthday.

We pulled in to the church parking lot and everybody got out of their cars, the van, or whatever, and we went inside and sat down in the nice little church. During the service, we heard the back door open and someone walking. We turned around to see Miss Kuhlman and her secretary Maggie. She loved Jimmy to the point that she made a special point to come and say happy birthday to him at his church. Knowing how busy she was and all the things that she had to manage, she took time to go out of her way to visit a friend. That was a big deal. That was compassion.

We all shared everything that Miss Kuhlman had—everything. I'm not talking about the dollars and cents and the houses. We shared the Spirit of God, every one of us. Every one of us were only led by the Spirit of God. It was an unspoken, mandatory element of the ministry; we followed only God's Spirit. We did not follow men or women. We did not follow things. We did not follow accolades. We did not follow any of that stuff. We followed the Spirit of God.

AND WE LAUGHED

Every day was a fun adventure during our times with the Kuhlman ministry. As mentioned previously, there were many life and death situations and suffering and pain before the healings, but there were also times to laugh and enjoy life. It's important to maintain a sense of humor while fulfilling the commission of Jesus. Believe me, we had no shortage of humorous experiences!

For example, while in Florida it was hot and our rented cars didn't have air conditioning. But one of the little elderly ladies traveling with us always wore a cotton house dress, thick cotton socks, and Oxford shoes. She had the typical temperament of a little old lady—she wanted her own way. One day, the little lady was sitting in the backseat and the retired engineer, who turned the nun's sheet music pages, was sitting beside her, sound asleep. Someone in the front seat opened the car window for some air, and when the wind rushed in, the little old lady's wig flew through the car and landed on the engineer's face. It was the funniest thing. We all laughed and laughed.

We experienced so much joy on those trips. They were really good times—compassionate times.

———— •◦• ————

Secret #4

COMPASSION RELEASES A MOVE OF GOD

You can actually release a move of God by being *moved* by the same thing Jesus was moved by—the compassion of God. The Gospels tell us that Jesus only did what He first saw His Father do. Time after time, we see Jesus being moved by compassion to heal the sick. This must mean that Jesus was motivated by the very emotions of His Father. The Father in Heaven is infinitely compassionate, and therefore Jesus healed the sick to show the world how good, kind, and compassionate the Father is. In the same way, when you share the healing presence of Jesus with those who are suffering, you make something invisible *visible*. The invisible God becomes visible as you step out in compassion and bring the power of Jesus to the hurting and broken.

———————•◦•———————

Chapter 8

Paying the Price for the Anointing

Kathryn Kuhlman talked about the concept of paying the price for the anointing. What does that mean? What does paying the price for the anointing look like? It is separating yourself from the world. That price means everything. It's not just a quick cost. It means that you are ready, willing, and able—with God's assistance—to live the life He designed for you. You're not a snob, you're not a stowaway. You live in the world but you are not part of it. You go to school. You rent or buy a house. You eat at a restaurant. You go to a movie. You go to the church of your choice.

You wear clothes. You try to look the best that you can. You choose to be different—to live a spiritual life, not a worldly life.

That price for the anointing means everything. It means that you are ready, willing, and able— with God's assistance—to live the life He designed for you.

Paying the price for the anointing of Jesus means we are separated from what the world has to offer. We're not prideful and we're not accusing. We're not judging people for what they do. Our hope is that something in our lives can show a better way.

Early on in life I saw a better way. I wasn't going to go down a bad road. I had a good family. Not one person in our family was ever a drunk. I had an uncle who went to prison. His wife had done something wrong, and he took the rap for it and he went to prison. He stayed in prison for about two years, and I remember seeing him in that prison as a little kid. Uncle

Nick didn't do it, but the authorities didn't know that his wife did it. He loved her so much he took the rap and they believed it, so he went to prison. That's compassion.

The price is surrendering our lives to Him—daily. We don't wear billboards saying look at me, I'm the best person on the block. It's more like having people look at us and see something wonderful that they would like to have for themselves. We are to be God's ambassadors. Others need to see in us someone who can solve problems. Christians are born to solve problems. They're not born to *be* problems; they're born to *solve* problems. They are people who can be approached and asked, "Will you pray for me? I'm sick, I need this," and we will take the time to pray for them. Christians need to agree with others in Jesus' name and watch things happen that only God can make happen. We can pray the prayer of salvation with people and agree in prayer for their wholeness and healing and study the Word with them—this is paying the price. We can live as close to Him as possible by obeying His commandments and following Jesus' example.

Miss Kuhlman paid the price in the example she lived. She didn't have a church-service face or demeanor as well as an everyday face or demeanor. She was the same in front of one person in her office as in front of thousands at a service. We are all tempted and easily slip off track, but she paid the price of her anointing by resisting every temptation and staying on track and on message—God's message.

That doesn't mean she didn't have fun. She was fun. She laughed. Even though she was known around the world (well, certainly nation-wide), she didn't allow that that to keep her from mingling with all people who came across her path. She didn't have to eat off gold plates. She ate off paper plates or whatever plates we were serving lunch or dinner on that day with the family. She was just one of the group—yet there was an aura around her that set her apart. She did not do anything to promote that; it was God's Holy Spirit living within her who set her apart.

She had no entourage around her other than her personal assistants, Maggie or Ruth. Some evangelists of the time were surrounded with numerous bodyguards. Not Kathryn. She had only Donnie who protected her at crusades. He didn't hang around with her otherwise; he just handled the people who tried to touch or grab her while on stage. He was a young, strong guy in the construction business. With "fame" came a degree of personal danger and inconvenience, but Miss Kuhlman accepted graciously that price to pay. She went to the airport by herself and flew commercial all the way until Oral Roberts let her use his airplane toward the end of her ministry.

Ultimately, paying the price means not having any worldliness. She loved what she did but she had to be careful—with her decisions, her words, her attitude, her clothing, her everything. She was a regular, normal human being who was watched constantly by everyone—friend and foe. Kathryn was representing God's Spirit. To do that, she had to be conscious of her every effort. No one can be who they were when they were born. Being in the spotlight, she had to be who He was inside; and there's a price to be paid for that.

Just a few examples—of course, Miss Kuhlman couldn't wear a scoop neck blouse exposing too much. Although she had a beautiful figure and could have worn anything, she dressed modestly. She didn't wear mink coats; I don't think she even owned one. She could have bought several of them, but that wasn't who she was. She lived in a small bungalow in a suburb of Pittsburgh. She drove her own car. She didn't have a chauffeur; but she did have a driver when traveling through some parts of the country. She hired a reformed alcoholic who came in off the street and gave his heart to the Lord. He drove for her until the day he died and was the only one who drove her car.

Normally, Kathryn drove herself. She dressed herself. She picked out her own clothes. She always wore her hair the same way—even though many thought it was unattractive. I don't think she even spent money at a hairdresser just to get it cut. I don't think she had perms or waves or had it styled. She was just a natural, lovely lady.

Miss Kuhlman was friendly too. She could talk to anybody and she was like their best friend. When you walked away from her, you felt like you had been with your best friend and you could reveal anything to her. Nothing was ever carried from person to person. She knew how to pray, and when she prayed the results were there. It wasn't like she had to fast or do this or that before she prayed. If someone was in need of prayer, she prayed for the person right then. She fasted a lot and she prayed a lot. She was continually in prayer but it wasn't like, "Let's dedicate this week to fasting for a new lamp." It wasn't like that. It was, "We pray and the needs are met; things come in." There was no conniving, no twisting the truth to get what was needed, no using sympathy to gather in what was needed. She was a woman of great integrity, and integrity is the result of paying the price for the anointing. A life under the influence of the Holy Spirit will shine forth the qualities of Jesus.

Kathryn stood for Jesus Christ. She stood for the Gospel. She stood for God's Holy Spirit— and the Holy Spirit and Miss Kuhlman were inseparable, which I think we all are, but He was her priority. She and the Spirit of God were one. She walked in His Spirit. She talked in His Spirit. Yet she was a person. I'm not saying she was a saint. There's no way she was a saint. But she was funny and cute.

She knew exactly what was going on in the world. She didn't hide herself from the news of the day. She knew it. She kept up on current events. She preached about them on her radio program and in her crusades. She preached all about what was going on in the world, especially what was happening in Israel; she preached it all the time. "Look at the newspapers. Oh, look at the Bible, it tells you what's going to happen," she would say.

WITHOUT HONOR EXCEPT...

Not everybody treasured Miss Kuhlman's life like those of us who knew her as an adult. Her neighbors in Concordia only knew the ornery little redheaded kid. She left, I think, before she was 16, and I know she had hard times. She preached. She slept in a chicken coop once. She slept on people's floors. She slept in chairs. And yet she just kept going. She was a human being, not a saint, and her life wasn't a bed of roses. And I don't think she ever thought of it like that.

She worked very hard all of her life to become someone who was known as being used by God to heal people—physically and spiritually. Before she became well known, she was out on the road, preaching on farms and in rural areas of Missouri and Illinois.

She was a giver. She wasn't a taker. When she met wealthy people and could have asked, pleaded, begged for money for the ministry, she didn't. She was gracious and allowed the Holy Spirit to control her words and actions. We introduced her to several wealthy people who could have easily provided much needed funds, but they didn't. Kathryn didn't sulk or become bitter—not in the least. She held her head high in glory to God and went about His business.

Ministries seem to always have struggles, but she never once said we're going to shut our doors. Miss Kuhlman never once said to the crowds, "If you don't send money, I'm going off the radar." Not once, because she didn't believe that. She was working for the God who provides, who does the impossible. Because of her ministry, treasures were deposited into people all around the world. Her anointing is her legacy.

Our city of St. Louis, has been changed forever because of the spiritual residue left behind by Kathryn Kuhlman. She favored St. Louis. She was here many different times, and each time many people were healed—body, mind, and spirit. She was a real Christian. A real Christian committed to God and all His children.

THE ANOINTING

Some have mentioned that when Kathryn was nearing the end of her life she began a transition, perhaps a mantle exchange. But I must say that I do not feel that I have her anointing.

Frank and I were with Miss Kuhlman for almost ten years and then we were with Benny Hinn for twenty-four years. We've laid hands on the sick everywhere in the world, not just in the United States. God has blessed us with so many amazing stories and experiences that if we thanked Him every moment of every day we still have on this earth, we wouldn't be finished showing Him our gratitude.

When we were first married, I remember the first night after our big wedding and we went to a hotel. When Frank laid next to me in that bed, we talked about the wedding and we talked about all of the people who were there. Then he turned to me and said, "Joan, we're going to travel the world."

And I thought, *OK, that sounds good to me.* At the time, I think he was making $99 a week as a mechanic at Goddard Motors in Jennings, Missouri, and I was a secretary there making about $69 a week. But every night that man would come to bed and say, "Joan, we're going to travel the world. We're going to see a lot of the world. We're going to do some stuff!" After a year and after two years, I would fall asleep before he said it. But what he said actually happened; we've traveled the world and laid our hands on the sick.

Financially, we don't have more than $200 in any bank account. We don't have things like that, but we've traveled the world and God has given us His greatest blessings. God has allowed us to eat the best foods, stay in the best hotels, go first class in airplanes or whatever mode of travel. People honor us when we arrive. We've never been rejected or turned away, and we've spread the Gospel of Jesus Christ. We have traveled the world and that's exactly what Frank said from the very first night we were together. I always believed that God fulfilled all of those things that Frank had an understanding of far before I ever did.

Now that we are toward the end of our time on earth, we thank God that our children are Christians and our grandchildren are Christians. We walk in the light of God's Spirit, and we've seen miraculous things happen all around the world according to God's will and way. We've laid hands on the sick and they have been healed. We've laid hands on presidents of countries and their wives and they were healed. God has been so very good to us.

Being involved with Kathryn Kuhlman and her ministry opened our eyes, our hearts, our spirits, and our minds to all that God had to show us and give us. We did what we could to assist her ministry, but it was the Spirit of God that kept the people coming and receiving from Him. The Holy Spirit drew people to her to learn how to yield to Him, not to worship her. She made people hungry for the Holy Spirit.

What greater gift of anointing could anyone ever bestow this side of Heaven?

FINAL THOUGHTS AND REFLECTIONS

So yes, Kathryn Kuhlman had a wonderful, unforgettable, impacting healing ministry. Most certainly her name will be listed in the history books among those in the twentieth century who were spiritual representatives of Jesus' healing ministry on earth. He never stopped healing people. Jesus never ceased performing miracles! Some might believe miracles ceased, but that is simply not so. The Bible says that *"Jesus Christ is the same yesterday, today, and forever"* (Heb. 13:8). His presence healed when He walked the earth, His presence healed through the first century church in the Book of Acts, and His presence still brings healing *today*.

Why offer you this volume on Kathryn Kuhlman? I want you to see how healing comes in His presence. Not through the presence of a person. Not through a celebrity. Not through some highly qualified, special individual. This was not Miss Kuhlman and this is not me either. Truly, Kathryn Kuhlman is special and set apart, not because of who she was naturally, but because of what *He* did through her.

Could it be that the very God who worked miracles through Kathryn Kuhlman wants to do the same thing through you? Don't for a minute think to yourself, "Well, I'm not Kathryn Kuhlman. I can't do *those* things."

The one writing to you is just as unqualified as *anyone* to walk in miracles, signs, and wonders. But I do. I'm unqualified to see food supernaturally multiply and the homeless get miraculously fed through our outreaches...but I see this happen regularly! It's not me, and it was not Kathryn Kuhlman. It's not *you* either. When we begin to get our eyes off of ourselves and on to Jesus, that is what qualifies us to walk in miracles.

Every one of the "secrets" that I've listed in this book is *not* something unique to Kathryn Kuhlman. They are transferable. You can practice them and actually experience supernatural results. Yes, Miss Kuhlman remains a hero in the faith for many. We give honor where honor is due, according to what the Scripture instructs (see Rom. 13:7).

---◦---

Secret #5
PAYING THE PRICE FOR
THE ANOINTING

Kathryn Kuhlman paid the price for
the anointing in her life. Even though
the Holy Spirit is a free gift given to
all who receive the work of Jesus, a
lifestyle of walking saturated in His
presence and filled with His power is
costly. It comes with a price. Yet what
we receive in exchange for what we
give up makes the price seem utterly
foolish. What we "give up" or "surrender" is absolute rubbish compared
to the gain of *knowing Christ*—the
Anointed One—through the per-
son of the Holy Spirit (see Phil. 3:8).
Whatever you pay for the anointing,
what you receive in return is what
Paul the apostle calls a *priceless gain*.

---◦---

So, how much do you want God to flow
through your life?

How much do you want to live saturated by
the Holy Spirit's glory?

How closely do you want to walk in fellowship with His wonderful presence?

It comes down to you simply saying a loud, consistent "yes" with your life. He's worth it. Trust me! Trust the stories I've shared from my experiences with Kathryn Kuhlman. Above all, trust the timeless words of the Scripture:

> *But what things were gain to me, these I have counted loss for Christ. Yet indeed I also count all things loss for the excellence of the knowledge of Christ Jesus my Lord, for whom I have suffered the loss of all things, and count them as rubbish, that I may gain Christ and be found in Him, not having my own righteousness, which is from the law, but that which is through faith in Christ, the righteousness which is from God by faith; that I may know Him and the power of His resurrection, and the fellowship of His sufferings, being conformed to His death* (Philippians 3:7-10).

✗ good

Concluding Prayers of

IMPARTATION
AND SALVATION

———•◦•———

Father God, I pray for every man, woman, and child who will ever read this book capturing the things that we have learned from Kathryn Kuhlman—a great woman You anointed and put Your hands on and used as an instrument and a tool to create in each of those she met, by the radio or in person, the desire for Your Spirit to live inside us as we saw in her. None of us want to be another Kathryn Kuhlman. None of us want to walk in her shoes, but what we do want, and I pray for those reading this book, is to just be themselves—the person You created them to be.

Reach out your hands and ask Him to make you as real as apple pie, to be as humble as the humblest in the land around, and to be as hungry as those who stood at Jesus' feet and wanted more and more and more.

> *God, bless each one of us with an understanding of Your Spirit that we've never, ever encountered before. Father, let us see the world around us as You see it. Father, help us realize that each one of us have born to be solutions in our land. Father, we haven't been born to bring troubles or to cause trouble or add to the trouble. We have been born again as Christians, Father God, willing to receive everything from You knowing that we lack in all these things, but with You living inside us nothing is impossible. God, we can ask in the name of Your Son Jesus to be filled with Your Spirit, to have the wisdom, Father God, that You've created us to have. And Father, please execute all the thoughts and all the hopes and all the desires that You've created in us. Father God, we reach out to You and we ask You, Father, fill us afresh and anew each day.*

God, let us not ask questions, but let us receive from You everything that we have need of and more and then share it with every living person. God, let us be the ones to forgive. God, let us be the ones to give. God, let us be the ones who are careful to reflect Your image. God, let us be the ones who spread the Gospel. What an honor it is. And Father, let all see in our lives Your Presence—not us, but You. Father, as we have seen and heard and walked with Kathryn Kuhlman through these pages, as we saw what she did from the platform, she knew and we know full well that it was by Your Holy Spirit that these things happened. Father God, let us yield to Your Spirit.

Fill us afresh and anew this day. A fresh baptism, Lord God, and we give You praise and we give You thanks all the days of our lives for what You are about to do with each one of us. As we lay hands on the sick, Father, they will recover. As we speak deliverance, they will be set free. Father God, give us Your wisdom. Let us walk in Your ways, not our ways, as we yield to You. Father, we thank You in the name of Jesus for the opportunity to serve You, to be called Your children. In the name of Jesus, Father, touch each one reading right now. Father God, bring life, bring health, heal the sick. Let the blind see. Let the deaf hear; let the lame walk.

Father, it's by Your Spirit. Father, we watched Kathryn Kuhlman walk out onto the platform time after time, not being afraid of what she saw in front of her because she could not do one thing to change any of it; her dependence was on You. She yielded to Your Spirit. She gave herself to You. "None of me and all of You" was said in every service. Father, none of us but all of You will meet the needs of everyone reading this book right now.

Dear reader, from the crown of your head to the soles of your feet, be made whole. Dare to stand up out of that wheelchair. Dare to open your eyes and see. Father God, touch ears and open them in the name of Jesus; heal each one who is deaf. And Father, those who cannot speak, let them speak; and those who are untaught, let them know, Father, that all gifts of wisdom are possible.

O Father, we praise You, we adore You. Father, we praise You. We praise You for touching every lost soul, every person who reads this book. To the very lost, the very sad, the very most needy, God, You can intervene. Reader, all you have to do is lift your hand toward Heaven and say, "Jesus, I need You. Jesus, I love You." Take Him into your heart right now. Ask Him to come in, wash you, cleanse you. There it goes! All the sin is being washed away, all the problems. Open your eyes, you can see. Turn your head, your ears can hear. Stand up from your wheelchair, you can walk in the name of Jesus. Nothing is impossible. Nothing is impossible. God is with you. In Jesus' name. Amen.

Father, I praise You. Father, we are so honored and so grateful for Your presence in our lives. Father, if we had a million years more to live, it could not be better than today. Today, Lord, we give You all. We yield ourselves to You, Father God. We surrender everything, Father. Everything we surrender to You. Thank You, Father, for receiving us.

Words we don't even know how to speak for the gratitude we should, we must shower on You. We could sit all day and speak Your name, God, that we could be in one accord, God, that we could experience Your Spirit like we are doing right now. Father, we shake with the excitement and the thrill and the gratitude of having 24/7 access to You, Father, through Your precious Son, Jesus. We yield ourselves to You, regardless of how many more years we have on earth. We're Yours, Father God.

O Father, there's never going to be a day like this in the rest of our lives. We're singing with the Spirit of God who lives inside us. Let us, too, do the things that have been spoken about in this book, Lord God. Let us touch the sick and they will recover. Let us speak freedom to the most captive of all, Father, and let them be set free. Father God, let us bring joy and happiness to everyone we meet. Father God, use our hands, use our eyes, use our arms, Father, to reach, touch, and hold.

O Father God, we praise You for where we are right now today. We praise You, Lord God, for what You've given us. We

accept Your love and mercy and grace
with open arms. Father, in the name of
Jesus, we surrender. We surrender ourselves to You. Thank You, Father, for
hearing our prayers, in the precious
name of our Savior Jesus.

AMEN, AMEN

What a Mighty God we serve !!!

ABOUT JOAN GIESON

Joan Gieson lives in an atmosphere of miracles and encourages everyone she meets to reach out and touch Jesus. After receiving a dramatic healing under Kathryn Kuhlman's ministry, Joan spent more than eight years working for Miss Kuhlman, transporting people to her healing services. Joan later became a key behind-the-scenes minister with Benny Hinn, traveling across eighteen countries, praying for the sick in his meetings.

Joan and her husband, Frank, reside in St. Louis, Missouri, where they are dedicated to providing shelter and jobs for the homeless through their organization, Ministries of Love.

MINISTRIES OF LOVE

---•◦•---

Learn more about Joan Gieson, her ministry with Kathryn Kuhlman and Benny Hinn, and her outreaches to the homeless and broken through Ministries of Love by visiting:

www.jgmol.com